YOU SEE BONE

To Isabel Paterson

who heard the ancient love song of the Lord
as an eight-year-old girl, and faithfully followed the music
to India. Isabel and her beloved Trevor served God for 13 years
in India. As a result, there are now over 4,000 churches
in the movement they began.

After Trevor was tragically killed in a car accident,
Isabel continued to serve God on many continents.
She has been a friend, mentor and spiritual mother
to many in All Nations.

YOU SEE BONES

FLOYD MCCLUNG

Unless otherwise indicated Bible quotations are the author's own translation.
NLT = New Living Translation
KJV = King James (Authorized) Version
NIV = New International Version
ISBN 978 1 842913 48 2

Cover design: PinnacleCreative.co.uk
Cover illustration: Howard Banks
Photography: © Roxana González/Dreamstime.com

David C Cook (UK)
KINGSWAY COMMUNICATIONS LTD
Lottbridge Drove, Eastbourne BN23 6NT, England.
Email: books@kingsway.co.uk

Printed in the USA

Contents

Foreword

Floyd McClung's books have changed my life.

The first time it happened, I was seventeen and struggling to make sense of my faith. I guess I was on a quest for an expression of Christianity altogether more dangerous than the Volvo-driving variety that pulled up politely, Sunday by Sunday, to populate the ancient pews of my local parish church. I was looking for a cause and I had a strong hunch that Jesus was 'it'. I wanted to find the Jesus who defied religious bigots with irreverent, funny stories; who kept bad company as if his reputation was of no importance; who had three years to save the planet and somehow found time to go to parties. I was attracted to the hilarious idea of the Creator God whose first miracle as a created being involved rather a lot of winemaking. I was impressed by the pacifist who went to the temple and breached the peace. I was looking for the revolutionary rabbi of Nazareth who (as far as the best biblical scholars can ascertain) never, ever drove a Volvo. I decided that, if it was possible to find this Jesus, I would follow him. But if I couldn't, if Christianity turned out to be mere 'moralistic, therapeutic deism' (as one author describes it), then I secretly planned to give up on church and have some fun.

God heard my cry and graciously sent me a couple of books. The first was Tony Campolo's *You Can Make a Difference* which said that a suburban adolescent like me really could change the world if I would just live simply, love Jesus and give my life to the poor. The second book – no less subversive – was Floyd McClung's international bestseller *The Father Heart of God*. Inspired by both books, I eventually climbed the North Downs and knelt by an old, wooden bench to do a very serious deal with God. I solemnly invited him to do anything – and I meant *anything* – to refine my character, so that I would be able to serve him completely. That wooden bench, where I knelt in the mud, was subsequently vandalized and eventually removed, but that moment of surrender impacts my life to this day.

The Master Plan

Several years later, I was studying theology and sociology at Greenwich University when Floyd McClung's writing impacted my life a second time. His autobiography *Living on the Devil's Doorstep* ignited in me a vision for participating in Christ's mission to the nations, and it also confronted me with an uncomfortable truth about myself. I began to realize that, if I was ever going to make a disciple of anyone, anywhere, I would first have to be discipled (not just trained) by someone somewhere.

'Disciple-making,' says Floyd in this book, 'does not just make a difference; it is the difference. It is the Master's plan.' If these were the words of a young firebrand, fresh on the footpath of faith, we could perhaps be forgiven a certain wry cynicism. But the really unsettling thing about this book is that every page, every insight, has been lived out and worked out over forty years at the coal face of pioneering mission.

As newly married twenty-somethings the McClungs established communities of faith on the hippy trail, publicly baptizing converts in Kabul, Afghanistan. There was widespread disillusionment with the conventional church, so Floyd and Sally responded by starting a trail of counter-cultural, Jesus-centred communities. Perhaps, in our era of similar disillusionment, we have lessons to learn from the quiet authority of such missionary practitioners who engage and experiment while others merely pontificate.

Passion undimmed

Now, forty years down the road from Kabul (via the Red Light District of Amsterdam, the mountains of Colorado and the plains of Kansas City), at an age when most couples are naturally thinking of easing up, Floyd and Sally's apostolic passion remains undimmed – perhaps it is stronger than ever. The McClungs have recently relocated to Cape Town, South Africa, to live in a simple church community as they oversee a movement of similar groups in over thirty nations. Floyd writes:

> I am determined to end my life more passionate than I began it. I want to finish on fire, more fiercely focused on following Jesus and living for his purposes in the earth than I was when I was twenty years old and trying to figure what my ministry was going to be . . . I am passionate; I dream about the nations being won for Christ but now I have the advantage of a lifetime of service to the Lord to give me perspective.

Simple church

You See Bones presents us unapologetically with the challenge of church-planting. The call to radical discipleship and mission to the nations found in Floyd's previous books is now firmly earthed in a radical understanding of church as the primary agency of the kingdom of God. This aspect of the book is, for me, its most exciting dimension. I believe that our generation needs to be released from the shackles of church politics in order to discover a truly missional, flexible, dynamic ecclesiology. *You See Bones* does not shy away from such controversy.

God is breathing on the dry bones of our generation; raising up the most unlikely people from the most unpromising places and turning us – even us – into a dangerous militia worthy of his name. In this book Floyd encourages and equips us practically to establish radical, simple communities of Jesus-centred faith all over the world.

Pete Greig
Guildford 2007

Five Beliefs that Changed the Way I Do Church

I believe in the church, but I also believe the church is in a crisis. The beginning point to solving a crisis is to see the need for change. It doesn't take a rocket scientist to figure out that the church in the West is no longer growing numerically, and has lost its ability to transform culture spiritually. That is a crisis.

People outside the church are interested in Jesus – but not in Jesus' wife. Sadly, the gospel is inseparable in those people's minds from the institutions of the church. Mega-churches are growing in many countries, and many of them are doing a great job of helping God's people. Churches like Moreleta Park NG and Harvest Church in South Africa, Saddleback and Willow Creek in the United States, and St Thomas Crookes and Hillsongs in England are great churches. I believe there is a strategic place for large resource churches.

But the size and number of mega-churches can give us a false impression if we are not careful. Overall, the number of people who attend church has rapidly decreased in Western cultures, while mega-churches have increased in size and prevalence. In other words, fewer people are going to church, but of those who do, the majority are attending large churches.

With this move to large churches, there is a simultaneous loss of impact on our culture. The church is no longer a transforming influence in Western nations.

I have a conviction: the way we do conventional church is no longer relevant to the vast majority of unchurched people in the West. Perhaps one of the reasons we have lost our relevance is because we spend so much time and energy thinking of ways to make the sacred hour on Sunday more attractive to saved people, rather than equipping saved people to take the church to the world.

Did Jesus die so we can build bigger buildings and print nicer bulletins? Or did he die to have a people that are so wildly in love with him that they share his passion to go into the world to win, gather and multiply more followers of Jesus?

No one will die for a cause that is no bigger than Sunday-oriented, building-fixated Christianity. But people will lay down their lives for a cause that is bigger than themselves, and bigger than the local church building. God created us to need a challenge so big it changes everything we believe and hold dear. He put us on the planet to have dominion over the whole earth. Only a dream that is daring in its scope and demanding in its call on people's lives will capture their imaginations and motivate them to live passionately to win the world to Jesus.

At the same time that we face a crisis of church relevance in the West, there is a spiritual revolution going on in the rest of the world. Millions of people are meeting in small home churches in China, India, Central Asia and South America. Without knowing it, they are breaking out of small definitions the rest of us in the West hold dear.

The 'rest' have a message for the West: church is not an institution but an army. Believers in the rest of the world are not devoted to doing church in religious buildings, but gathering anywhere and everywhere they can to study the words of Jesus and to pray and worship. The participants in this revolution believe they are at their best when they meet in twos and threes, not two-and three-thousands. And they don't see their small gatherings as the purpose for church, but the means for them to be encouraged in their longing to see more people know Jesus.

The followers of Jesus around the world who do church in small, simple organic communities believe Jesus is continuing in them what he came to begin 2,000 years ago. They believe they don't have to be ordained to lead, that they were called when they said yes to following Jesus, and all they need is a Bible not a Bible school. They don't believe they need to have a theological education to understand what Jesus was up to when he said to 'go into all the world and preach the gospel'.[1] They believe that what Jesus taught and modelled about church is simple enough that anyone can do it.

What Jesus taught about church is so simple *anyone can do it*. His example of doing church was a community of men and women reaching out together. Because of what Jesus modelled and taught about church, I call it simple church. I don't think one model of church is better than any other, but I do believe the more complicated we do church, the more difficult it is to reproduce. Complicated ways of doing church are overwhelming and difficult to feel part of. How many people believe they can start or lead a mega-church?

Success in doing church, as defined by Western methods of church, is often counter to birthing a spontaneously reproducing movement of churches. In other words, we can build big churches, but is that the best way to reach the most people? As Neil Cole says, 'Most Christians today are trying to figure out how to bring lost people to Jesus. The key to starting churches that reproduce spontaneously is to be Jesus to lost people.'[2]

A word about models of church: I am much more interested in what goes into the model than the model itself. I believe any model of church that wins, gathers and multiplies followers of

---

[1] Mark 16:15

[2] Cole, Neil, *Organic Church*, Jossey-Bass (Wiley) 2005, p 24.

Jesus is a good model. But the fact is that, the more complicated and bigger a local church becomes, the more people and the more money it takes to lead one person to Christ.

I have spent most of my adult years living and working outside the United States. I travelled extensively for four years in the West Indies; I lived for eighteen years in Europe, three years in Afghanistan, and now I live in Africa. I have served both inside and outside conventional church structures. I have served as the pastor of a mega-church. I worked for many years in one of the fastest growing and most vibrant missionary organizations in the world. Now I am involved in a network of simple-church-planting movements spread out around the world. I am nurturing a church-planting movement of simple churches in townships in South Africa, and training others to do the same. My perspective is one of love and loyalty to the church of Jesus Christ, but not to any particular way of doing church. Though I live in Africa, I carry the world in my heart. There are over three billion people on our planet who have never heard the name of Jesus spoken to them one time. I ask myself, why should some people hear the name 'Jesus' over and over again when there are so many who have never heard his name once? There remain thousands of people groups that have not been reached with the good news of God's grace. Poverty, corruption, preventable diseases and famine have turned whole countries and continents to ruin in our global community. I am stirred to face these challenges with faith in God's goodness and obedience to his commands, especially his last command to make disciples in all nations.

What do I believe theologically? I believe in the orthodoxy of a radical community of Jesus-followers who seek to alleviate injustice and share the Father's love with those who have never heard that he cares for them. I believe the church of Jesus Christ is the hope of the world. Jesus himself chose the church to be his ongoing, incarnate presence in the world. I believe anything good that comes through the church is from Jesus and for Jesus.

I believe God has a big dream, but I also believe he transforms the world one life, one family and one community at a time. I believe in dreaming big and building small, one new *ecclesia* of believers at a time. I believe the effectiveness of any movement that makes a lasting impact will be measured by how effective it is in fostering a culture of discipleship that thrusts its members out among the lost.

By living out my beliefs and passing them on to others I am pioneering what will become, by God's grace, a movement of simple churches in two poor communities in Cape Town. My dream is for a movement of culturally relevant churches that impact every aspect of people's lives. I dream of a discipleship culture that changes lives and transforms the communities we serve.

I began this book by asking myself this question: What are the most important life-lessons I have learned in regards to church, leadership and mission? If I were to try to pass on to a handful of disciples or leaders the most important core beliefs I have learned about leadership, church and mission, what would they be? After reflection, I boiled everything down to five foundational core beliefs. I have focused on these five non-negotiables because they are the inner beliefs that serve as a grid for how I interpret the teachings of Jesus, determine what risks I take, and guide the decisions I make.

I concluded many years ago that all followers of Jesus interpret the teachings of Jesus and the impressions of the Spirit via an inner set of core beliefs that, for better or worse, guide their lives. These five guide my life:

- Simple church
- Courageous leadership
- Focused obedience
- Apostolic passion
- Making disciples

As I expand on these five core beliefs in the pages that follow, I pray that what has been passed on to me will inspire and encourage you to re-imagine church, and in the process empower you to experience the Spirit of God breathing on the dry bones of your dreams.

His church is an army. Sometimes we see the bones, but when his Spirit breathes on the bones, we see an army. I invite you to join me on my journey.

Floyd McClung
Cape Town 2007

I SEE

by Jonathan David Helser and Shane Key[1]

I SEE A MOUNTAIN, YOU SEE A MIRACLE
I SEE A WASTELAND, YOU SEE A GARDEN
I SEE DRY BONES, YOU SEE AN ARMY
I SEE IMPOSSIBLE, YOU SEE EVERYTHING

YOU ARE, I AM,
BUT I'VE BEEN SO BLIND ALL THIS TIME
MY GOD, TOUCH ME,
I WANT TO SEE THE WAY THAT YOU SEE

I SEE A SEED, YOU SEE A HARVEST
I SEE THE WATER, YOU SEE THE WINE
I SEE THE BROKEN, YOU SEE THE BODY
I SEE MY ENEMY, YOU SEE YOUR FOOTSTOOL

I SEE MY SIN, YOU SEE THE BLOOD
I SEE A BABY, YOU SEE A SAVIOR
I SEE MY FAILURE, YOU SEE REDEMPTION
I SEE A BEGGAR, YOU SEE A SON

I SEE MY FATHER, YOU SEE YOUR SON
I SEE MY SHEPHERD, YOU SEE YOUR LAMB
I SEE MY SAVIOR, YOU SEE YOUR JOY
I SEE YOUR EYES, STARING AT MINE

God Grabbed Me

'God's Spirit took me up and set me down in the middle of an open plain strewn with bones. He led me around and among them—a lot of bones! There were bones all over the plain—dry bones, bleached by the sun. He said to me, "Son of man, can these bones live?" I said, "Master God, only you know that." He said to me, "Prophesy over these bones: 'Dry bones, listen to the Message of God!'"

God, the Master, told the dry bones, "Watch this: I'm bringing the breath of life to you and you'll come to life. I'll attach sinews to you, put meat on your bones, cover you with skin, and breathe life into you. You'll come alive and you'll realize that I am God!"

I prophesied just as I'd been commanded. As I prophesied, there was a sound and, oh, rustling! The bones moved and came together, bone to bone. I kept watching. Sinews formed, then muscles on the bones, then skin stretched over them. But they had no breath in them.

He said to me, "Prophesy to the breath. Prophesy, son of man. Tell the breath, 'God, the Master, says, Come from the four winds. Come, breath. Breathe on these slain bodies. Breathe life!'"

So I prophesied, just as he commanded me. The breath entered them and they came alive! They stood up on their feet, a huge army.'[1]

---

[1] Ezekiel 37:1–11, *The Message,* © Eugene H. Petersen 1993, 1994, 1995 by NavPress, USA.

PART ONE
Simple Church

1

Holy Frustration

The church is God's idea

I discovered early on in life that I loved Jesus, respected my parents, but disliked church. Church for me was predictable, emotional, and out of touch with the real world. The best way to describe my experience of church is to tell you about a film I saw a few years ago called *Instinct*. But before I do that, let me give you a little background.

I grew up in church. My father was a pastor. In fact, I come from a long line of preachers. As a member of the youth group, I was urged to 'bring your friends to church'. I tried that once. It was a disaster. I brought one of my best friends with me to a 'revival meeting', a pal named Gary Miskey. Gary was a tall basketball player like me. We hung out a lot, practised together, and were both too shy to date. So we ate, drank and slept basketball. That was basically our life. When Gary finally gave in to my pleas to attend one of our church meetings, it was hard on our friendship. The service was great as far as Pentecostal services go. People danced, shouted, clapped their hands, and worshipped God joyfully. But it freaked Gary out. For a Lutheran like Gary, it was too much. Our friendship survived my guilt-induced invitation to 'go to church', but after that he thought I was a little weird.

Our friendship survived my guilt-induced invitation to 'go to church', but after that he thought I was a little weird.

By the time I went away to university I was totally put off by church. I was tired of meetings, especially super-sized, over-the-top worship times and preachers who preached at people instead of talking to them from their hearts. I got to the place where I could spot a religious person a mile away. They had the God voice down really well. They had this kind of warble in their voice when they prayed, and they raised their voice like God was hard of hearing.

Fortunately, I met some real guys in my dorm at university who genuinely loved Jesus. Church for me became late-night prayer meetings with my friends, early morning devotions with one of the guys in the residence hall, and weekly worship times with the guys I hung out with.

I had a good experience of church in Afghanistan. I didn't go there to find church, but you could say it found me.

I had a good experience of church in Afghanistan. I didn't go there to find church, but you could say it found me. We rented a big house in Kabul and opened our home to anyone in need or just curious about what a bunch of 'Jesus-freaks' were doing in Afghanistan. We were there to help dropped-out Western backpackers, people who got sick, who lost their passports, or worse, got strung out on drugs. We ran a free clinic and teahouse downtown, and took in the homeless and strung-out 'world travellers' as they were called.

Kabul was not a good place to get sick. You could catch more diseases in the local hospital than you got rid of. Soon, we had

20 to 30 people living with us at a time. We rented more houses to take everyone in. Hundreds of internationals got to know Jesus over the few years we lived in Afghanistan.

We shared our meals together, played football and developed a routine of prayer and Bible study before we did work projects or visited people in the prisons and hospitals. When people came to live with us, we didn't insist they believe what we believed, but we did ask them to follow our routines of prayer, work and common meals. We put a lot of effort into a caring, personal mealtime. We took turns serving each other so the meals were not too chaotic. It was not unusual to have 20 or 30 guests eating with us. At the end of the meal we read a few verses from the words of Jesus and discussed what they meant. We welcomed anyone to make a contribution. Then we sat around the table afterwards, drank chai and talked. People were fascinated with our life together. Many of them became followers of Jesus simply by observing our lifestyle of community and care for each other.

I realized one day that what we were doing was church. We didn't call it that. There wasn't a sign outside that read 'First Church of the Hippies' but we were doing what they did in the book of Acts. I had rebelled against the idea of church, but now found myself leading a community that was in fact a simple church, based in our home.

I took a big step forward in loving 'the church' on a teaching trip to Europe. I had been invited to give a week of lectures at a training centre in Lausanne, Switzerland. I had responded to an invitation to spend a week teaching the students on how to tell people about their faith in Jesus. While there, I spent time alone in the little guest room in the afternoons. I decided to read the book of Ephesians. As I read Paul's words, I became profoundly aware that I didn't see the church the way Paul did. I reflected on my cynicism about everything I had seen in the church. The great apostle's words in Ephesians 3:10 sounded really far-fetched to me:

'. . .that the manifold wisdom of God might be made known by the church . . .'

I tried to understand what the words meant. I looked up the word 'manifold' in a dictionary. It means 'varied, many different kinds, having many parts'. The question that followed for me was, how could a perfect God make known the many and varied aspects of his greatness through imperfect people? As I struggled with what Paul was describing to the Ephesians, I had a distinct impression of God speaking to my mind, like one of those silent conversations we have with ourselves. I know this sounds far-fetched, but I had an impression of God speaking to me these words: 'This is my greatness, to make myself known through the people who are my church.' It didn't make sense to me. But I had the distinct impression that what I was hearing was one of the greatest things I would ever learn about God. I reflected on the implications of what he was speaking to my heart. It seemed like he spoke to me again: 'That I reveal myself through broken, fallen people is a revelation of the God I am.'

How could a perfect God make known the many and varied aspects of his greatness through imperfect people?

Slowly, the revelation grew in my mind. I had seen plenty of the church's problems, but God seemed to be saying to me that it is actually part of his plan to welcome broken, weak people to be part of his family, the church. I began to really understand for the very first time that God invites us, as the church, to partner with him in revealing his love to others. That he chooses to partner with us even though we are sinful is a sign of his greatness. I am still stunned by God's humility and kindness. That he invites me to be a co-worker in sharing his love with others never ceases to amaze me. Obviously, this throws a new light on what the church is about.

It's important to get this right. Sooner or later, someone will do something to hurt us or disappoint us, and we will once again have good reason to avoid 'the church'. Dietrich Bonhoeffer points out in his book, *Life Together*, that the church is not a comfortable place for idealists and humanists. Church is a community of forgiven sinners, a family of people who need mercy from those who have learned to forgive like Jesus.

I am an advocate of simple church. But simple church is not a panacea for all that ails the church. Every church is made up of people, and people are fallen. Fallen people hurt and disappoint each other. We make mistakes. We sin. The closer we get to each other, the more we see each other's faults, and the more we can hurt each other. If we seek community with other followers of Jesus without an orientation to forgiveness and mercy, we will experience continual conflict and division. We will struggle to trust other people, as if their sinfulness is the problem. Sin is not the greatest barrier to community, but lack of humility is. Sin in others is not the greatest barrier to unity, but idealism about our own sins is. Idealistic humanists don't do well in a community, not because they are not perfect, but because they have not acknowledged their imperfections and received the forgiveness of God. If they have not received forgiveness, they will struggle to give it to others.

> **Sin is not the greatest barrier to community, but lack of humility is.**

Doing church like they did in the book of Acts

In the months that followed my experience in Switzerland, I read about the church in the book of Acts with new eyes. I saw what the church could be today. I read about a church that shared their possessions with one another. I saw in my mind's eye a church that was vibrant, growing, and courageous. It was a community of people who were wildly in love with Jesus, not an institution devoted to buildings and programmes. I saw friends eating meals in one another's homes and remembering the Lord's death as they celebrated communion together. I saw them worshipping with whatever musical instruments they could find, making joyful sounds as they praised God for sending his Messiah. In my mind's eye I saw pictures of small communities of believers spontaneously multiplying all over Jerusalem: the teachers, prophets and evangelists in their midst moving between the home-based communities of believers, making sure they stayed connected to one another. The apostles and prophets laid the right foundations to build on by instructing and encouraging the believers.

The church in the book of Acts functioned as a vibrant community, not a weekly meeting. It was a church of little churches, or more accurately, a movement of churches. They certainly were not a mega-church, as we understand it today. They were a dynamic movement of small communities, spontaneously breaking out all over the city. They occasionally met together in big celebrations in Solomon's Porch at the Temple. They gathered in each other's homes, crowding into living rooms and gardens and workshops, wherever they could find space to gather and worship and pray for their friends and family. They were infiltrating every part of the city.

> *They certainly were not a mega-church, as we understand it today. They were a dynamic movement of small communities, spontaneously breaking out all over the city.*

Think about the power of what was happening: they often spent times fasting and worshipping and speaking words of encouragement to one another.[1] They preached boldly about Jesus. Common people were discovering unknown abilities to teach, pray for the sick, serve and organize. Everyone was involved. The whole church was actively engaged, not just a few. The simple model of gathering in small communities lent itself to everyone's involvement. Their way of life was attractive to those they came in contact with. How could it not be, since what the people had known for years was the impersonal and oppressive authority of the Pharisees? God had breathed on the dry bones of Judaism, and an army of ordinary people came to life. It was 'an army of the ordinary' called out by the stirring of God in their hearts.

Holy frustration with unholy church

I began by saying there is a film that portrays a picture of church that I identify with. A lady I respect a lot gave the DVD *Instinct* to me. She invited Sally and me to meet her in a restaurant near where we lived at the time. She had a copy of the film in her hand. She told us a simple story about the film, and how it related to our lives. Her story aroused our curiosity but at the same time made me a little cautious. 'Where is she going with this?' I thought.

She had gone to see the film with her husband a few months before, and as they sat down in the theatre her eyes filled with tears. 'There was no natural reason for me to cry. I just started crying,' she told us. 'I had the impression while waiting for the film to begin that God was going to speak to me. After I watched the film, and had some time to reflect on what happened, I felt I was to buy a copy of the film on DVD and give it to you, Floyd. So here it is.'

I was startled. Maybe apprehensive is more like it. Did *Instinct* contain a message from God for me, as she implied? I waited several days before I watched *Instinct*. I wanted to have undisturbed time to take it in. So I set aside an evening, turned off my mobile phone, and settled in to enjoy it.

---

[1] Acts 13:1–3

The tale told in *Instinct* is set in Harmony Bay, a prison hospital for the mentally insane. A rising young star in the world of psychiatry, Dr Calder (played by Cuba Gooding), is given a once-in-a-lifetime opportunity to interview a former professor-cum-mentor who is being repatriated to the United States for two murders he allegedly committed while on a research project in Africa. Dr Ethan Powell (played by Anthony Hopkins) is being detained in Harmony Bay to undergo observation before his trial.

As I watched *Instinct* I recognized a modern day parable of the church. The story is about community, authority, and the value of spiritual mentors. It may seem unconventional to learn something about the church from a Hollywood movie, but the storytellers of our day often give us insight into the human predicament and the need for redemption. There is a deep longing in the human heart for beauty, mystery and community. Like the church, *Instinct* touches on those longings.

> *There is a deep longing in the human heart for beauty, mystery and community.*

What does that have to do with the church? Sadly, institutional churches do not explore those longings. Christianity as embodied in conventional churches is increasingly viewed by the postmodern world as the least likely option for those seeking a relational, artistic, politically subversive and activist kind of faith. Earlier in the film Dr Powell confronted the young Dr Calder in a very intense and dramatic scene, forcing him to face the secret fears that drove him.

As a result, the young doctor becomes a force for change in Harmony Bay. A subversive community begins to form around him. He is only one man, and though he has no position or recognized authority in the prison hospital, his desire for honesty and his willingness to stand up to institutional authorities has a profound impact on the inmates. Injustice is confronted, and as a result the prisoners begin to experience hope. The community of half-crazies and psychopaths that forms in Harmony Bay teaches us about belonging, transformation, and resistance to authority that does not serve.

Towards the end of the film, the young Dr Calder opens his heart to Dr Powell: 'You asked me a question once. "What has you all tied up in knots when you wake up sweating in the middle of the night?"'

The young doctor continues, 'I've been thinking about it a lot. It's not the work. I love the work.

'It's the game. It's the game, Ethan. I was so good at it.

'I made sure all the right people liked me. At night I did the checklist in my mind. Am I cool with Ben Hillard? Am I cool with Dr Josephson? Am I cool with all the people who can help me? Am I cool with all the people who can hurt me? Anybody who is weak or is a loser? Anybody I was offending?'

Then Dr Calder pauses and reveals his heart: 'I loved that game. But guess what? You taught me how to live outside the game. You taught me how to live...'

The ambitious Dr Calder has found a friend and teacher in a man supposedly in need of his help. Through his contact with Dr Powell he is forced to face his fears, as well as the lies he believed that empowered those fears. As a result, he experiences freedom. He works inside a prison but now his own heart is free. He heals broken people, but more importantly, he has learned to receive healing for his own heart from those he serves. He is part of community now, not just someone who fixes people. He is a leader because he leads by serving people, not by serving his own agenda for the people. He helps the inmates believe in themselves, to speak out, to care for each other, and to experience real freedom for themselves and others in Harmony Bay.

I was drawn to the message of *Instinct*. I saw the church with all its foibles and weirdness – the church I once despised but have now come to love. The church I am part of. I saw myself in Dr

Calder: ambitious, driven, self-aware, and yes, filled with vision and a desire to make a difference. I also saw in Dr Calder what I wanted to be: a man willing to challenge the status quo.

Sadly, the church is more often like a prison than a healing community, with its hierarchies and political games. I saw in the story of Harmony Bay the broken but beautiful church of Jesus Christ. Local churches can easily become a spiritual Harmony Bay, locking people up instead of setting them free; with church leaders who mean well, but if they are not led by the Spirit their efforts can turn the church into a world unto itself, cut off from reality.

Outside the walls of the church are hundreds of millions of people suffering in poverty, dying with AIDS, abused by gender injustice, and exploited by wars and corruption. The church that does not carry a passion to reach the world isolates people behind walls of cultural irrelevance. When that happens, pastors and leaders serve like guards on the prison walls instead of liberators sent to pull down the walls. They stand as caretakers of dry-bone cemeteries, instead of speaking life to the dry bones.

The church that does not carry a passion to reach the world isolates people behind walls of cultural irrelevance.

The very word for church in the New Testament is about an empowered citizenry commissioned to lead, not control. The word *ecclesia* meant much more to its audience 2,000 years ago than it does to us today. *Ecclesia*, or church, did not convey a Sunday meeting to go to, or a boring, building-oriented place where a few people did all the ministry and everyone else was a spectator. William Barclay explains what the word *ecclesia* meant to the early disciples:

> It was a convened assembly of all the citizens of a city . . . the ecclesia directed the policy of the city. It declared wars, made peace, contracted treaties and arranged alliances. It elected generals and other military officers. It assigned troops to different campaigns and

dispatched them from the city. It was ultimately responsible for the conduct of all military operations . . . Its two great watchwords were 'equality' and 'freedom'. It was an assembly where everyone had an equal right and equal duty to take part.[2]

The ecclesia was the power centre of culture and life. It was the ecclesia that directed the affairs of the city. They were at the centre of things, not the prisoners of a walled-off asylum. No wonder Jesus came back to set his people free from the religious leaders of the day. They had turned Judaism into a religious club controlled by a few old men instead of the liberating army of God sent to declare wars and assign the troops to their battle stations.

I was also drawn to the message of Instinct because I grew up in a church tradition that was not unlike Harmony Bay. There were exceptions, but generally my church was out of touch with the world. As a young visionary, I became suspicious of institutional structures and religious leaders who could preach amazing sermons but were not marching in the streets against injustice. I wanted to face the future with imagination and courage while the traditions I grew up with encouraged people to react to anyone who challenged the status quo.

My journey led me eventually to start a street ministry to dropped-out young people. My wife, Sally, and I saw ourselves as part of the same revolution that was started by Jesus and the early church. We were unafraid to critique institutional church traditions, even though we weren't sure where the revolution was leading us. I left my church because it was out of touch with reality. While my friends were taking part in civil rights demonstrations, my church was busy drawing up more rules.

So I left the church as a young man, and signed up with Youth With a Mission, a radical Christian organization that was mobilizing

---

[2] This definition is taken from a book by Vishal Mangalwadi called The Truth About Justice and Social Reform (Good Books 1996). The definition itself comes from Barclay's book, New Testament Words (SCM Press 1964).

young people to go to the nations. I wanted a challenge and they gave it to me. But, as radical as we were, we were still tied to the irrelevant practices of conventional churches. Sally and I led a street ministry in those days, so that meant rousing our converts out of bed on Sunday mornings so they could 'go to church'. We functioned like the church in the book of Acts all week long, but on Sunday mornings we had to pretend we were not church so we could go to church! Unfortunately, the churches didn't know what to do with our tattooed, pierced disciples. It was a battle every Sunday morning. I experienced a growing disillusionment with this practice. Church as we experienced it one morning a week was not relevant to the young people we were reaching and the city we lived in. I was deeply frustrated.

> *Church as we experienced it one morning a week was not relevant to the young people we were reaching and the city we lived in.*

At the same time, I was dreaming about doing church the way I read about it in the book of Acts. Fortunately, a spiritual mentor came for a visit and I took the opportunity to seek his counsel. I told him about my frustrations, that I wanted to do church differently, but I wasn't sure how to do it. He smiled like he knew something I didn't know, then told me God had given me a 'holy frustration' to get me ready for change. He told me that frustration creates energy, and if I would steer that energy in the right direction, it would lead to new ideas and new ways of imagining church. He encouraged me not to focus on the things that frustrated me, or on what I disagreed with, but to see God at work in our circumstances to prepare us for something new. 'God is giving you a new vision,' he said. 'He has lifted his grace off you to live with the way things have been to get you ready for the new thing God wants you to do. It's God's way of preparing you for changing the way you do church.'

I walked away from that conversation full of hope. I started seeing my frustration from a positive perspective. I started dreaming about a new way of doing church. What I dreamed about was so different from how I experienced church that I didn't dare call it church. Like a lot of leaders, I made the mistake of putting the 'church' in a small box in my way of thinking. It was not the creative, subversive movement Jesus started, but a meeting on Sunday to attend.

A few months later a Bible teacher came to Amsterdam, where we worked at the time, to conduct a seminar for us. After seeing what we were doing in the city, he commended us for the many young people we were leading to Christ, but then he asked why we didn't gather them and start an alternative church. He said to me, 'You are blessing many young people, Floyd, but what are you building?' When I asked him what he meant, he talked about the responsibility of being a spiritual father to the young people that were coming to Christ through our ministry. I was barely old enough to vote, how was I to be their father? He told me that Sally and I should not expect others to take care of those we were leading to Christ. He challenged us to gather them in small groups, and as we were able, in celebrations. He called this process 'building' in contrast to 'blessing'. He told me that doing ministry without a clear aim to build a healthy community, an *ecclesia*, was irresponsible. He said God had something better in mind. He challenged me to build a discipling community that we led and cared for, and in turn, became part of God's mission.

> *You are blessing many people, but what are you building?*

His words struck a deep chord in me. We were blessing the local churches to a degree, but in the process we were losing many of the young people who didn't fit in the churches we were attending. We behaved like we were *ecclesia* all week long, but then on

Sundays we pretended we were not really God's *ecclesia*. This confused everyone: those who were seeking our assistance, the local churches, and ourselves most of all. The young people we were reaching out to were confused because we were confused. We lacked a clear vision of who we were. Were we church or weren't we? And was the radical community of young disciples we led an army or just disconnected dry bones?

The challenge of this spiritual father led me to consider a new way of thinking about church, and the role I was to play. The building versus blessing paradigm revolutionized my thinking about God's *ecclesia*. Blessing other people is good for all of us, but leaders in God's church are called to partner with Jesus in building his church. Paul tells us in 1 Corinthians 3:10 that he was a 'wise master builder'. In this passage Paul describes his building paradigm in these terms:

- he built on the right foundation – Jesus Christ
- he built with gold, silver and precious stones – with people
- he built with the correct plans – establishing an *ecclesia* wherever he went
- he built with eternal perspective – an eternal reward
- he built in the 'field' – outside the walls of religious systems

The question of building versus blessing was forced on me in my early days of following Jesus because the young people I was reaching didn't fit in conventional local churches. They had a different culture, a different way of dress, and a different way of thinking. It was like we were trying to force two different cultures into being one. I came to the conclusion that we were abandoning the young men and women God had given to us by trying to bless the local churches in town. God had deposited things in us that he wanted us to impart to those we were reaching out to. They were our spiritual sons and daughters and we were to impart our spiritual DNA to them.

We had prayed many times for fruit in what we did, and when

it came, we gave it away. We taught our values to the young people during the week, but then implied by our actions they were not the radical *ecclesia* we read about in Acts. We were teaching by our example on Sundays that a church building was where 'real' church took place. There was an inevitable conflict between the values and vision we taught and what the local churches were teaching. We had a deep longing to be a father and mother to the young people we were leading to Christ, but we weren't sure where our responsibility stopped and the local church's started. Who did have responsibility to disciple our converts? Were we responsible? If so, why were we sending them to churches that didn't have that responsibility? I came to the conclusion that we were putting our spiritual children up for adoption, but without their permission.

We were putting our spiritual children up for adoption, but without their permission.

I bought into the building paradigm of ministry because I saw the weaknesses of blessing without building radical New Testament *ecclesia*. To help you understand the difference between the two paradigms, you could compare them like this:

By transitioning to a building paradigm I went from a meeting mentality to a movement framework of thinking. I transitioned from a youth ministry of keeping people happy, to establishing a radical *ecclesia*. We were fashioning an army out of dry bones. As I look back now, I can see with hindsight that God was calling us to build his church. But because we saw ourselves as an extension of existing churches, rather than pioneers of new church communities, we had the wrong framework for what God was calling us to. Every apostolic leader must face this challenge: will I build what God has called me to build, or will I extend what others are doing? You want to know why potential apostolic leaders don't make this transition successfully? Lack of courage. God lifts his

Building Paradigm	Blessing Paradigm
Focused	Following spiritual fads
Strategic	Lost in church culture
Intentional	No clear outcome
Building a movement	Living for the moment
Pioneering spirit	Pleasing others
Long-term thinking	Short-term mentality
Fruit that remains	Immediate results
Fathers and mothers	Hirelings
Building spiritual foundations	Adding to what others do
Values-oriented	Meeting-oriented
Spiritual sons and daughters	Crowds and meetings
Reproduction	Production

grace off church leaders to get them frustrated enough with the old way of doing things so they seek a new way of doing church.

God wants to change everything about how we view church. He cares for the old, but injects new life into his church through those people who are courageous enough to change. As a young man, I read and dreamt a lot about radical Christian community, but until I took courage and lived my dream, I didn't discover the new things God wanted to teach me. Dry bones don't live again if they keep lying on the ground. They have to rise up and march.

I wish I could tell you there was a quick and radical breakthrough in what I was doing, and as a result our work grew quickly into a church of 5,000 people. I am envious of those who preach from the book of Leviticus every Sunday for the first year they start a new church, and after twelve months they have a church of 10,000 people. It does happen, but not for me. My journey was much slower, and was marked by many stops and starts. I made a lot of mistakes. Fortunately, God helped me to learn from my mistakes. One of the things I committed to was to do nothing that did not lead to new church communities being started. The results were amazing. We started churches among the prostitutes and in unreached neighbourhoods. New churches sprang up as a result of our efforts in Central Asia, Russia, India, Mongolia and Greece.

> *We started churches among the prostitutes and in unreached neighbourhoods. New churches sprang up as a result of our efforts in Central Asia, Russia, India, Mongolia and Greece.*

God blessed our efforts. One leader we discipled in a small Bible study group went on to start a movement of churches that has grown to over 40 congregations in several nations. Another young man we invested in impacted the youth of a whole nation through music and arts festivals that are now influencing tens of thousands of unchurched young people. Scores of new church communities have risen from this ministry.

A story of unending and glorious victories

Did I mention that my life has been one unending and glorious victory? Would you believe me if I said that? Of course you wouldn't, and you shouldn't believe anyone else who gives that impression. When I told the pastors of the churches we had been attending that we wanted to start new churches, they reacted. In fact, I didn't meet one leader in the city who encouraged me as a young visionary to dream about starting new churches. They were concerned with losing church members. They felt the city didn't need more churches. They felt our vision was too big, that we were getting our ideas from America, not God. Some of these leaders were inside the walls of 'Harmony Bay' and were doing their best to guard the prison from attack. They were good men at heart, but they were locked into a way of thinking about church that was narrow, and sometimes controlling. I decided I didn't want to be the kind of leader that reacted unfavourably to young visionaries.

What Sally and I did build was unconventional but not un-biblical. By withdrawing from the churches we shifted from a strategy of revitalizing existing churches to one of reformation of how we did church. We were getting in touch with God's desire for us to impact the culture around us as the reason for our existence. I believe we were tapping into the primal evangelical urge of the Spirit of God for the good news to be given to the world. I believe God wanted us to reach the outsiders, not coddle the insiders. We stumbled on the apostolic nature and calling of the church.

What beat in my heart then is the same stirring in the hearts of many emerging leaders now. It is a latent desire stirred by the Holy Spirit for the *ecclesia* to be unleashed. It is the creative presence of the Holy Spirit yearning for a community of people who will engage their culture and reach their world. It is the Spirit calling us to live the gospel *within* our culture, rather than perpetuate church institutions that exist *apart* from our culture.

My journey has convinced me that it is time for a new kind of Christianity. Not in reaction to the church, or church leaders, but because the *ecclesia* is called to rise up and live, and because there are so many people who will never 'go to church'. It is time to bypass outdated institutions that occupy people with irrelevant focus. I say this, not because it is fashionable to be anti-church, or because I don't love the church, but because the salvation of the church is to be found in the church's apostolic mandate. The Holy Spirit yearns to make Jesus real and known in our world. The best way, in fact the only way, to renew the church is for a fresh apostolic imagination to be unleashed in the church.

> The best way, in fact the only way, to renew the church is for a fresh imagination to be unleashed in the church. It is time to bypass outdated institutions that occupy people with irrelevant focus.

As I have travelled the world, I have found that the ministries which lack resources and credibility are often the very ones that have the most to offer in terms of creativity and inspiration. What they lack in money and status is made up for by courage and vision. I didn't know it then, but what we were doing when we pioneered new churches and helped others do the same was a form of protest, not against dead liberalism, but against dead evangelicalism. Those churches were dead, not because of wrong beliefs, but because of wrong practices and wrong values. The church had retreated from the world it was called to reach.

We became a force for change in the city of Amsterdam by embracing God's heart to reach out. When we started there were five to ten churches that were preaching the gospel and engaging the culture. Today, including simple churches that meet in homes, there are over 400 churches in the city. And they are impacting the city in a significant fashion.

Asking the right questions about church

Most people are asking the wrong questions about church. How do I grow my church bigger? How can our church become more relevant to the world? Or even worse, 'How many people attend your church?' These are questions that lead us in the wrong direction.

We have to get to the core of the issue. If we don't define church the way Jesus defined it, we won't just build on the wrong foundation – we will build the wrong building altogether!

We have to start with the core issue about church, and that is, what is church? Or to put it the way a friend asked me many years ago, 'What are the minimum biblical essentials to *be* church?' This is followed up by two other crucial questions, 'What is the purpose of church?' and 'How do we do church in a way that causes people to grow, the lost to be won, and the Lord to be glorified?' To summarize:

What is church?
  What is the purpose of church?
    How do we do church?

By asking these three questions, we allow ourselves to look at the church in ways we may have never seen before. That takes courage. When we do that, we are really seeking a fresh definition for the meaning of the gospel. By answering these three questions with fresh imagination for yourself, you will get at the heart of what the *ecclesia* is called to be. If you don't answer those questions for yourself, you can spend years experiencing the same 'holy frustration' I experienced. You can spend a lifetime 'blessing' without building something lasting. If you are not careful, you will end up maintaining a spiritual hospital cut off from reality instead of leading an *ecclesia* made up of people on fire for God.

The answers to these three questions will differ for each generation. I am not writing this book because I have found the formula for doing church the right way. There are models of church that I am excited about, but the model that works for me is not the answer for everyone. In fact, no one model will reach the whole world. We need more than new models; we need a new paradigm of church and the right core values to empower us to live what we believe. You can add candles and artists to the Sunday programme and still be working out of an old paradigm of church. And you can reduce the big meeting on Sunday to a small meeting on Wednesday, and not really change anything but the size of what you do. The challenge before us is major reformation, not tweaking the meeting format. The Spirit of God calls each generation to re-imagine church for their own context and culture, and to a fresh encounter with God to live the gospel. Every generation needs to struggle to discover answers and approaches for themselves about church, answers that bring them into fresh partnership with God and fresh contact with their culture and their world.

> *The challenge before us is major reformation, not tweaking the meeting format.*

Answering the three questions mentioned above is part of both encountering God and rediscovering God's calling to be his *ecclesia*. God invites us to partner with him and his mission by creating new wineskins. If you are frustrated with church, it could be God's way of trying to get your attention. Holy frustration is God's way of leading us to fresh life. As I relate my journey I will tell you some of the answers I came up with as I wrestled with these questions, but I encourage you to seek your own answers. Try to imagine what church would look like if it was a powerful force for change in the lives of people you relate to.

There is a great danger of defining church according to our past experience or dry theological explanations. Describing church is not the same as defining it. And once we ask the right questions, we must be open to the unexpected. God has created the church to be a dynamic, growing, powerful movement, not a static doctrine. Don't let past traditions box you in. The Holy Spirit invites every generation and every race of people to create new expressions of church. Jesus called these new expressions 'wineskins'. This is part of the adventure of being the church. Father takes a lot of joy in allowing us to create with him. I found out that it was God who was the one behind my frustration when I went through this creative process. He wanted me to break out of the old ways and find new ways of doing church and, in the process, discover the power that was latent in the church. He was challenging me because he wanted to breathe new life into the dry bones of church as I experienced it and as I defined it. He will do the same for you if you let him.

Don't try to fix the church. God is not calling us to fix what he has created. Don't focus on changing the people and the churches they are part of. All the people who want a 'fixed' church have already found one. It is time for a new wave of church leaders to be released who do church in brand-new ways. Old traditions don't suit new needs. As you read this book, I hope you hear the Spirit speaking to you. God may be calling you to believe him for your generation and your culture. Dare to believe him for a new way of thinking and a new way of acting, based on God's word and infused by God's Spirit.

New ways of doing church must be born on our knees, out of desperation for God. What is born on earth must first be conceived in heaven in the place of prayer. If God is driving you to himself through holy frustration, it is in his presence that you will experience a new revelation of his church as the army he wants it to be. Get alone with God. Cry out to him. Weep out of desperation. Then heaven will come to earth. Jesus taught us to pray, 'Your will be done on earth as it is in *heaven*.' We desperately need heaven to come to earth. It is his will, his desire to do so. With this confidence we can pray urgent, sincere prayers for him to breathe life and power on the dry bones.

2

Asking the Right Questions

What is church?

Is it too simplistic to think we can define church in a few words? Is it possible for untrained non-experts to grasp what church is about? Some theologians would have us believe that it's impossible to describe in a few words what they have spent whole volumes trying to define and describe. But from my perspective, it's possible to define the church in a few words because that's what Jesus did. Theologians have made church far too complicated. The Bible defines church very simply because God wants everyone to be part of it. Jesus came not only to die on the cross for our sins, but to give the church back to ordinary people. That's one of the reasons he made us all 'leaders' in the church. You don't have to go to a Bible school for four years to be a leader in the church. In fact, Jesus defined leaders in the new way of doing things as servants. If leaders are servants, anyone who serves God's people through their gifts, leads.

In the religious systems of his day, religious rulers used religion to control people. When Jesus came he turned everything on its head: he made *everyone* who believed in him a leader. Tax collectors, fishermen, political terrorists, Roman officers, men and women alike. Everyone was invited to be part of the church. It was the *ecclesia*, the 'convened assembly of all the citizens of a city. . .'

It is possible to define the church in a few words because that is precisely what Jesus did.

One example of this radical change God was bringing about was when the church first came to Europe. It started in the home of a woman, actually a businesswoman. Her name was Lydia. Paul heard about a group of God-fearing women meeting to pray by the riverside outside Philippi. Not very remarkable to our Western way of thinking, but in the first century this was a radical departure from the religious practices of the Jews and the Greeks. Lydia responded to Paul's preaching with a trusting heart, and thus became the functional leader of the first church started on the European continent.

If your way of thinking about church is institutional and doctrinal, you may be tempted to patronize Lydia's role as a woman and minimize her importance, but if you think of the *ecclesia* like Jesus defined it, you will believe that God very intentionally used a woman to lead the first church started in Europe. It was a simple church that met in her home, and that's exactly how God wanted it. Nothing fancy, just a community of people built around the leadership gifts of a businesswoman who opened her home to Paul and his co-workers.[1]

Though Paul pioneered the first church in Europe, it was Jesus who modelled simple church, and defined church in such simple terms. He did this to help his followers understand the new way of doing things. Here is the way Jesus defined church:

'Where two or three are gathered in my name, there I am in the midst of them.'[2]

---

[1] Acts 16:14–40   [2] Matthew 18:20

Church happened for Jesus and the twelve as they formed a community that learned and lived and served together. It happened when Paul told a women's prayer meeting in Philippi the good news. It happens today when a family invites a few friends over for a meal on a regular basis. As they eat and break bread, they build a spiritual community together. They are the church gathered. When they seek to obey the commands of Jesus together, they are a church with clear purpose. When several like-minded communities band together, there you have a fellowship of small communities, growing together in a shared vision. Like Vineyard Central in Norwood, Ohio. They describe themselves as a 'community of home churches'. They speak about their church gathering in 'size small' and 'size large', in home churches and monthly celebrations.[3]

Let me try to give a little more substance to the definition of church from Matthew 18:20. It's important to note that the definition given by Jesus was in the context of restoring people who have strayed from the faith:

○ '. . .*two or three*. . .' It doesn't take a crowd, just a few people to be church and fulfil the functions of church. Jesus was clarifying that he wants each of us to be connected with a few others in intentional community. The small size keeps it simple, relational, reproducible, easily hidden in places where persecution arises, and not too difficult to organize. 'Two or three' implies that Jesus had a clear idea in mind of the church being small and organic.

I believe in simple church for several reasons. I love big churches as well as small. One is not better than the other. In fact, both are necessary and share equally in God's plan for the church. But if you have to reduce it down to the barest essentials, a small church is able to keep on going when all else fails. Further, small groups of Jesus-followers are easily reproducible.

---

[3] See www.vineyardcentral.com to learn more about this innovative church.

People can't hide or get lost in a small community. Caring for one another is made easier because everyone knows each other. And lastly, I believe in simple church because simple expressions of church, like a cell group or a house church, can function in closer proximity to those who don't know Jesus by meeting in homes, businesses, on campuses, etc.

The context of Matthew 18:20 is restoring people who are spiritually lost. Jewish tradition required ten men to constitute a synagogue or even hold a public prayer meeting. But Jesus does away with this man-made requirement. He promises to be with even *two or three* people, male or female, who gather to restore those who are lost, not just ten men. The truth that Jesus is teaching about 'two or three' is not just applicable to church discipline. He is teaching a new way, a new order of things. No longer is it ten or more, no longer is it men, and no longer does it have to solely be for the purpose of discipline. Jesus promises to be present with his flock (notice his reference to lost sheep in the verses preceding verse 18), even if it is just two or three, as long as they gather in his name and live for his purposes. Nothing more is required. There is more that will be helpful to the growth of the *ecclesia*, but not more that is required.

○ '. . .*gather together*. . .' To gather is to build community. To gather is to invest in one another's lives through personal accountability and discipleship. To gather is more than a happenstance meeting with other followers of Jesus. There is more structure and form to gathering than a spontaneous type of 'hanging out' at the local pub or coffee shop when it suits our fancy. To gather implies commitment; it speaks of building a spiritual family. To gather includes celebrations, where people join together for worship, the study of God's word, outreach, and for prayer and doing life together. Acts 2:42–47 illustrates how followers of Jesus gathered from house to house as small, committed communities that loved and obeyed Jesus together.

○ *'. . .in his name. . .'* The church is made up of those who seek to know, love and obey Jesus. By gathering 'in his name' we are committing to more than attending a weekly meeting. We are pledging our allegiance to him. To be gathered *in Jesus' name* means he is first, he is the one we gather for and about. He is the centre, the focus.

All told, Jesus gave over 30 commands in the four Gospels. Those who gather 'in his name' seek to study and obey those commands. Consistent with this truth, Acts 5:32 tells us that the Holy Spirit is given to '. . .them that obey him.'

What are the commands of Jesus we are to obey? The commands of Jesus can be summarized in these seven imperatives:

1. Repent, believe and be baptized.
2. Love God and others.
3. Give your resources and finances.
4. Forgive each other.
5. Pray and worship together.
6. Live a holy life.
7. Go and make disciples.

Not that complicated. The *ecclesia* are those committed to obedience. Obedience to the commands of Jesus sets us apart. Followers of Jesus become fully devoted disciples when they get serious about obeying Jesus' commands. The goal of church is to help followers of Jesus to become obedient disciples of Jesus.

○ *'. . .there I am in the midst of them. . .'* Jesus promises to be with those who obey him. When he gave the first disciples the commission to go, teach, baptize and make disciples in all nations, he told them to teach others the things he commanded them.[4] He wanted them to pass on the commission he had just given them.

---

4 Matthew 28:19–20

Jesus didn't say we had to gather on a certain day, or in large numbers, or that a recognized pastor/leader had to lead us, or that we had to be 'under the covering' of a recognized leader's spiritual authority, although those things can be very helpful if done in the right spirit. Jesus defined church in the simplest of terms. He made church available to everyone. There is a place for large churches and recognized leaders, but church is not built on the recognition or approval of any human being or dependent on any human institution. The church of the living God is his idea – we are gathered by God himself.

When God's Spirit breathes, things begin to happen. The dry bones start to get up and dance. We know it is the *ecclesia* we read about in Acts because of how it dances and battles and lives life.

Ecclesia is committed community. It is doing life together with others. It is about shared meals together, telling friends and neighbours about Jesus together, hanging out together, laughing and crying together, and growing together through transparency with others committed to loving and following Jesus.

Ecclesia is family. We are the family of God on earth, the overflow of the family of God in heaven. The Trinity is family. The church is family: the Father sent the Son and the Spirit to create on earth what they enjoyed in heaven. As the family of God, we are named after the Father, 'from whom every family in heaven and earth is named.'[5] 'Family' may not be a positive word for those who had negative experiences growing up. We have the opportunity to change the word and make it positive. We get to enjoy family at its best: we belong, we are unconditionally accepted, we know with certainty we are loved, we receive a new identity, and we learn to receive loving discipline and correction. Jesus did not die for the idea of world evangelization, he died for people, he died to create a family of sons and daughters.

---

[5] Ephesians 3:14–15

Ecclesia is an army. It's an army of dry bones come to life. God's Spirit can turn a disconnected, dead and lifeless bunch of bones into a cohesive community of lovers of Jesus, marching in unison. Armies are for war. God's army is at war. But our fight is not against people. The 'bad guys' we war against are not terrorists, or abortionists, or liberal politicians or seminary theologians who deny the virgin birth of Christ. Our war is not a culture war with the right or the left, nor is it a war against fundamentalists or racists. God's army is an army of love, empowered to fight against poverty, injustice, corruption and greed. God's army is held together with kindness, not hate. The focus of our battle is against spiritual forces of evil, sometimes embodied in evil people, but they must never become our focus lest we become like the ones we resent.

> *Our war is not a culture war with the right or the left*

The war between conservative and liberal Christians in most countries would go away overnight if the *ecclesia* occupied itself with demonstrating the love of Jesus to the poor and marginalized rather than speaking against people we disagree with. The war against racism, corruption, poverty and crime in our world would go away quickly if all God's people would stand together against the evil that is destroying people's lives. We don't have to agree on everything to stand together for something. God's dry-bones army wins battles by recognizing our need for one another. We win battles by fighting in the opposite spirit. Instead of violence, we fight with peace. Instead of anger and hate, we fight with love and forgiveness. Instead of power, we fight with humility. Instead of demanding our rights, we fight with meekness and transparency. Our weapons are not those made with human hands, but they are fashioned in the hearts of humble people.

I am convinced the church needs to fight its way creatively out of the missional and spiritual malaise it is in. We need a revolution, a second reformation. We don't need more faddish theories of church growth, or more conferences or books about new techniques to attract or integrate people. But we do need a new understanding of church and a fresh empowering of God's Spirit. The church needs to fundamentally reform itself. We need a revolutionary new approach to being and doing church. Not a franchise approach that produces cookie-cutter clone churches, but a commitment to build God's kingdom on earth. We need a new set of values, a new vision, and a new way of thinking. Such a focus of serving and engaging our culture will continually drive humble and fearless people to their knees in dependence on God for fresh outpourings of the Spirit.

> *A focus of serving and engaging our culture will continually drive humble and fearless people to their knees in dependence on God for fresh outpourings of the Spirit.*

The failure of the church to fulfil its mission is a problem that requires a fresh wave of creativity and imagination. The same thinking that created our problems is not going to solve them. Michael Frost and Alan Hirsch quote Albert Einstein as saying, 'The kind of thinking that will solve the world's problems will be of a different order to the kind of thinking that created those problems in the first place.'[6] Frost and Hirsch go on to point out that Einstein was a paradigm shifter. He thought with such originality and creativity that his ideas 'precipitated no less than two, and some argue three, major paradigm shifts in our understanding of physics and of the cosmos, and in so doing changed the

---

[6] Michael Frost and Alan Hirsch, *The Shaping of Things to Come*, Hendrickson 2003, p 7.

course of history and shaped the thinking of generations.' There are many who believe the same kind of 'paradigm-busting' imagination is desperately needed if the church is to be all we are created to be.

Five paradigm shifters for doing church in a new way[7]

To grasp the stunning implications of the mandate God has given us to 'disciple all nations. . .'[8] we have to break from many of the old ways of doing church. The cultural expressions of Christianity have failed to transform our culture. Look around you. . . two million babies die of malaria in Africa every year while we build bigger and better buildings. We are losing the war on AIDS. Drugs are consuming our youth. We have to transition to a new way of thinking about church or we will become the laughing stock of the world. I believe that understanding God's view of his church will only be discovered when we address core issues of justice and spirituality, leadership and mission. There has to be a fundamental change in the DNA of our thinking about these issues, a shift away from dualistic spirituality, institutional views of church, exclusive attitudes of who can lead or belong, hierarchical leadership structures, and attractional approaches to the mission of the church.

> *Two million babies die of malaria every year while we build bigger and better buildings.*

I believe the five paradigm-busting principles concerning church shared below can help us break out of the old way of doing church that imprisons us. Church leaders and serious followers of

---

[7] Adapted from *The Shaping of Things to Come.*
[8] Matthew 28:19–20

Jesus who want to make a difference in their continent and in the world will find themselves at home with these principles. They are not new, just not applied. I share them with the conviction that we are the fruit of God's encounter with humanity, and that God wants us to take up these principles and live them. They are the pillars of his kingdom. They are:

1. Holistic versus dualistic spirituality
2. Apostolic versus hierarchical leadership
3. Incarnational versus attractional mission
4. Simple versus institutional church
5. Inclusive versus exclusive membership

Holistic versus dualistic spirituality

Holistic spirituality affirms all of life as a gift from God to steward and offer back to him as worship. For example, those with a holistic spirituality see their work as a holy calling. In that respect, we can never hire enough pastors and missionaries to change the world. We need a few more rock musicians like Bono. Being 'full time' for God is not about being 'called' to a religious vocation or 'the mission field' but realizing that no matter what our vocation or where we live, we are called to represent the heart of God and share the love of Jesus 'full time'. Holistic spirituality means that making money and earning a living is not the primary purpose of any occupation, but 'being there' for God, active, subversive, and courageous, is our calling and purpose.

> *Holistic spirituality affirms all of life as a gift from God to steward and offer back to him as worship.*

Holistic spirituality means we don't limit church to one day a week, but we see ourselves as church in the world every day of the week. A holistic paradigm allows us to see ourselves as the church in the world, enjoying life, celebrating and worshipping every day of the week, on mission with God to influence people in the sphere of life we are in. It is interesting to note that most of the covenants in the Bible ended with a meal, including wine and dancing. In the same way, God's covenant with us as his people is to be celebrated regularly with meals and joyful laughter and, if one is able, a little dance. To our enjoyment and to God's glory, worship, mission and celebrating life are all integrated in holistic spirituality. A dualistic view of the world sees the church as one sphere of life and 'my work' as another sphere. This paradigm says the church is to stay separate from the world. I picture this unfortunate paradigm of church and world like this:

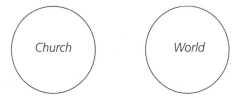

To carry this illustration a step further, a dualistic spirituality leads to a self-centred paradigm of self-seeking spiritual experiences. It helps me to picture the results of dualistic spirituality like this:

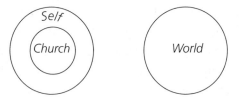

In contrast to dualistic spirituality, a holistic paradigm of the church, self and the world looks like this:

When we make the shift from a dualistic to a holistic paradigm of spirituality, we move from passive to active spirituality. In fact, we must question any form of spirituality that does not lead to action. Only holistic spirituality offers the opportunity to sanctify the ordinary and 'make daily connections between heaven and earth'.[9] What most people today are looking for is not a more perfect church or a better theology, but a more purposeful and relational expression of church to be part of in the face of a haphazard and chaotic world. Fully devoted disciples of Jesus want to be part of something greater than themselves. A church community that is on fire for God offers people an opportunity to belong to what they were created to be part of: a community gathered in his name and living for his purposes. In short, that radical *ecclesia* we have been speaking of.

Apostolic versus hierarchical leadership

Hierarchical leadership is based on position, title and power. It is a command-and-control model of church that operates like a top-down company. Management models of how to lead church break down at this point. The church is an organic, reproducing movement. To follow a formal process to recognize leaders in the church is not inherently wrong. But human tendency is to institutionalize the way we do things. When that happens we make maintenance of established structures our focus rather than risk-taking advancement and innovation. Without apostolic leadership the church is unlikely to risk at all and, when it does, it lacks the conviction and commitment to sustain the advances made in the first place. I devote more attention to what I mean by apostolic leadership in a later chapter, but I would like to briefly frame what apostolic leadership is and how such leadership works in the church, so the reader has a context for my proposals for change.

---

[9] *Ibid*, p 145.

If the church is to be the army of God, it needs servant-hearted generals who impart passion and vision. I use the term *apostolic* specifically to refer to visionary leadership that provides energy and creativity, as well as missional initiatives. In referring to apostolic leadership I do not have in mind the top-down, big-hero model of leadership favoured by many charismatic and evangelical leaders today. Apostolic leaders will lead, but that does not mean they have to manifest a type of religious tone of voice or carry themselves in such a way as to say, 'I am the boss around here.'

> **If the church is to be the army of God, it needs servant-hearted generals who impart passion and vision.**

An apostolic church is a church that is gripped by the imperatives of Jesus to preach good news and plant new communities of faith.[10] Apostolic leaders are missional, that is, they align themselves with the mission of God. An apostolic leader is one that believes the whole church is a sent church. Their defining values are to win, gather and multiply kingdom-minded communities that reach unchurched people, impact culture and touch nations. Apostolic leadership is God's mechanism for mobilizing his people. It is a tragedy that, for most of the church's 2,000-year history, apostolic leaders (I include evangelists in this statement) have been made itinerant, and therefore marginalized from the life of healthy local churches. Institutional churches have ignored the role of the evangelist, prophet and apostle. Pastors and teachers have had more than their share of recognition. It's time to restore greater balance to all five of the equipping gifts that

---

[10] The disciple-making process that Jesus outlined was simple but deliberate: go, teach, baptize and make. Baptizing implies initiation into a community of common faith, the church. Local churches were formed naturally as a result of gathering with others who believed in Jesus when his followers followed this four-step process.

Paul describes in Ephesians 4, but not in a top-down, command-and-control structure.[11]

How does apostolic leadership function in a simple-church movement? By pioneering new communities and ministries that are aimed at reaching those outside the church. Faithful apostolic leadership is not given by God to reproduce more programmes for Christians, or to tell people what they can and cannot do for God, but to reach those who are not yet following Jesus. There is a place for recognized spiritual authority, but that authority is relational not hierarchical.

Apostolic leaders are groundbreakers and strategists who initiate new endeavours to 'go where no one has gone before'. They work in the marketplace as well as in the nations. They are entrepreneurs and innovators. Ideally, apostolic leaders focus their creative energies, not just on the activity of creating something new, but on the ultimate goal of pioneering and that is reaching and gathering followers of Jesus who are discipled to reach others also. The ultimate purpose of the apostolic gift is gathering those who come to faith in Jesus into vibrant, reproducing, obedient communities of faith.

> **The ultimate purpose of the apostolic gift is gathering those who come to faith in Jesus into vibrant, reproducing, obedient communities of faith.**

One of the primary ways God uses apostolic leaders is to gather people around shared vision and values. Hierarchical leaders favour the neatness and predictability of institutional structures, but apostolic leaders prefer to build movements. Movements are dynamic, fluid and growing. They are messy on the edges but

[11] For an excellent presentation on the biblical basis and role of all five equipping gifts in the life of the church, see Michael Frost and Alan Hirsch, *The Shaping of Things to Come*, pp 164–180.

have energy at the centre. A movement is an attitude, a mindset that says, 'We are not going to wait for history to happen, or watch it happen, we are going to make it happen.'

Hierarchical leaders focus on control, order and nostalgia. Apostolic leadership yearns for the 'not yet'. Dreaming, faith, imagination, risk taking, pioneering and future goals characterize apostolic leadership. Administration, bureaucracy, reminiscence and impersonal systems and structures characterize hierarchical leadership. Apostolic leaders encourage holy dissatisfaction, risk taking, questioning and experimenting.

Apostolic leaders can also serve as hierarchical leaders, but they do so to their own detriment. They were not made by God to oversee organizational bureaucracy. They were not designed to manage, but to lead change. I have found personally that to the degree I am caught up in maintaining church structures, something in me dies. My creative gifts and energy turn inward and I am less effective in every way. I battle with the balance between initiating new efforts to reach the lost, and maintaining what I initiate. But I know from failure and past experience that I need to be involved in reaching those who don't know Jesus if I am to keep the balance right.

Paul was an apostle, and as such, functioned as a visionary leader. He held to independent views and refused to conform to the religious structures of his day. He was a maverick. We need to make space for apostolic mavericks like Paul in the church today. It is the visionary mavericks that play a vital role in questioning the status quo. They propose mind-blowing alternatives to how things have always been done. Michael Frost and Alan Hirsch make this profound statement about the role of biblical mavericks: 'In a real sense, a true biblical maverick acts in a prophetic manner by exposing the lies that the dominant group tells itself in order to sustain its shared illusions. . .'[12] Amen.

---

[12] Michael Frost and Alan Hirsch, *The Shaping of Things to Come*, p 195.

Incarnational versus attractional mission

Jesus was God incarnated among us. He lived a simple life, learned a common trade and spoke a human language. He toiled with his hands to provide for his mother and brothers. He was in his culture. He was fully divine, yet he did not allow his divine rights or prerogatives to overwhelm how he related to ordinary human beings. He did life. He sanctified the ordinary. He did not live from one spiritual high to the next. He suffered, experienced frustration, endured hardship, and waited for the right way and the right time to fulfil the will of his Father in heaven. He lived purposefully but in the context of ordinary work and family and fun. He lived life intentionally. He validated ordinary life to sanctify ordinary life for the rest of us. He lived an integrated type of spirituality.

The incarnation is absolutely fundamental to understanding our mission in the world. Not just the mission of the 'missionaries' but all of us. All of us who obediently follow Jesus are on mission with God. We can all draw inspiration and wisdom from how Jesus came, lived, worked and reproduced his life in others. The incarnation allowed Jesus to *identify* with people. It provided a way to *localize* and live out his calling. He made God *available* in his neighbourhood, so to speak.

To apply the incarnation principle to our life situation, we must recognize that Jesus was a genuine part of people's lives without doing damage to their culture. By living in a culture he affirmed the worth of that culture. David Bosch says in his book, *Transforming Mission*, that it should not bother us that the Christian faith is lived out in different ways in different cultures. Bosch says, 'The Christian faith is intrinsically incarnational.'[13] What this means is that we should not export churchy, Western styles or Korean styles or African styles to others. That would be a 'distortion

---

[13] Quoted in Michael Frost and Alan Hirsch, *The Shaping of Things to Come*, p 37.

of the incarnational principle of mission.'[14] The same could be said about various sub-cultures as well. Every culture, every sub-culture and every generation must discover for themselves how be true to their culture while being fully obedient to Jesus.

Being incarnational means relating to people in ways that allow us to identify with people without compromising our message. The great danger of failing to *incarnate the gospel* is cultural imperialism – imposing our culture on people in the name of God. The great danger of failing to *proclaim the gospel* is to imply that cultures and peoples do not need to be transformed by the power of the good news. Not only is this true from one culture to another, but from the church to the non-churched. Many people cannot relate to Jesus because they simply cannot relate to those who speak 'Christianese' – and the churchy way they act.

> **People need freedom to discover Jesus on the inside of their culture, not in an imposed culture from the outside.**

The incarnational approach implies that it is not necessary to extract people from their culture in order to be faithful followers of Jesus. Christians love to extract people out of their context and surround them with 'Christian' music, dress, friends and activity. We want to protect them and guard them from falling, from persecution and from friends who will have a 'bad influence' on them. Surely this indicates a lack of trust in the Holy Spirit? And why is it we think this way about drug addicts but not about bankers? Paul didn't extract his converts from their culture. Nor did Jesus. Paul preached, gathered the new believers, taught and baptized them, and then trusted the Holy Spirit in them to empower them to live their faith in their culture, not apart from it. Rolland Allen points out in his book, *The Spontaneous Expansion*

---

[14] *Ibid*, p 37.

of the Church,[15] that a lack of trust in the Holy Spirit is what separates church planters today from Paul and his day. Paul's greatness was his radical trust in the Spirit of God to keep those who believed in Jesus inside their culture, not removed from it. It was not his signs and wonders, or ability to speak different languages, or his eloquence in debating with the Jewish leaders and Greek philosophers of his day that made Paul a great pioneer. It was his simple trust in God in people. People need freedom to discover Jesus on the inside of their culture, not in an imposed culture from the outside.

The attractional approach to church is about improving our programmes, projecting better audio-visuals, and getting people to come to our church instead of the church down the street. It caters to the consumer mentality of 'shopping around' to find the church we like best, that 'fits us'. There are church growth conferences dedicated to better car-parks and more appealing children's programmes. When I hear people talking like this I feel what Jesus must have felt like when he cleansed the Temple. What have we come to? Better car-parks? The right packaging of our worship set? Is church really that far gone in our Western ways of doing things?

Jesus modelled for us the way to do church: among the people. He said it clearly, 'As the Father sent me, in the same manner I am sending you.'[16] Church is not for us. It is for God and for the lost. God created us to glorify him and to take his love to others. We are part of the church because God was gracious enough to forgive us and invite us to join him in reaching out to those who don't know Jesus.

Simple versus complicated church

The church of Jesus Christ is first of all a family, a community. The basic unit of church life is a small group of people, as small as two

---

[15] Rolland Allen, *The Spontaneous Expansion of the Church*, Eerdmans c.1962.
[16] John 20:21

or three people. God himself is a family – Father, Son and Holy Spirit. God began the first expression of *ecclesia* with a man and woman, Adam and Eve, and told them to multiply. The Bible often speaks of the power of two or three people. It says, '. . .by the mouths of two or three witnesses a matter will be established.'[17] Jesus sent out his disciples in groups of two or three. He said where two or three were gathered in his name, he would be with them.[18] I believe there are distinct advantages to such a simple expression of church and ministry:

1. *It is simpler to get things done.* It doesn't take a long time to conduct the business meeting of the church!
2. *Accountability is more natural and powerful with two or three people.*[19] It is more difficult to confess sins or weaknesses with a larger group of people.
3. *There is greater flexibility.* It doesn't take as long, or involve as many decisions, to change or adapt to new opportunities.
4. *Communication flows more easily with a small group of people.* Misunderstandings can be cleared up more quickly when the group is smaller.
5. *There is greater proximity to people who don't know Jesus.* It is natural for a small group to meet in a restaurant or bar or office, thus keeping a group located among people who don't know Jesus.
6. *Direction is more quickly and clearly confirmed in simple church.* God often uses two or three others to confirm what he says to us.
7. *Leadership has to stay natural and relational.* When the leadership functions in a small group of people, it is much more difficult for it to function from a lofty 'position', since everyone knows each other.

[17] Deuteronomy 19:15

[18] Matthew 18:20   [19] 1 Timothy 5:19

8. *Multiplication can happen spontaneously as the group grows*. It doesn't take a worship band, a fat cheque, a telemarketing campaign and a new building to plant a new church!

God's *ecclesia* is simple, not only because it is small, but because it has reduced the primary purpose of church to reach and disciple and multiply followers of Jesus in such a way as to be a transforming presence. Simple church does not depend on paid pastors to lead the people, religious buildings to gather in, and well-run programmes to entertain and care for the people. These things may not be bad in and of themselves. They are bad when they hinder initiative, responsibility and confidence in people's hearts. Simple church seeks to empower people by avoiding bureaucracy, dependence on buildings, hierarchy, and 'come to us' models of mission. Simple church spontaneously and deliberately gets everyone involved – where they live, play and work.

> **Simple church spontaneously and deliberately gets everyone involved.**

A friend of mine in the States told me recently about a failed attempt to start a simple church. He is a gifted teacher, so naturally he wanted to teach. In the middle of a long monologue in one of their early gatherings, one of those present interrupted him and said, 'If I wanted to sit and listen to someone talk the whole time we are together, I would have stayed in the church I attended every Sunday. I'm here to be involved, not watch you do everything!' Simple church emphasizes a facilitative style of leadership that aims at getting everyone involved, and every person's gifts identified and mobilized by reaching out to the lost. The difference between complicated church and simple church is that the complicated church relies on programmes to disciple people, while simple church empowers people to disciple people.

Church is inclusive not exclusive in nature

The fifth paradigm buster that radically changes the way we do things is to actively seek out those who are spiritually open, no matter their status, colour, gender, or where they are on the journey towards Jesus. Jesus' way of doing things was to treat women as equals, men as friends, Romans as examples of great faith, and lepers as recipients of his love. He sowed the seed of the kingdom indiscriminately and abundantly, and then challenged those who wanted to know more to 'get in the boat' and become disciples.[20]

When we pass rules about who can become part of our community, or who can teach or lead, we are thinking like brain surgeons, not followers of Jesus. Church is a loving family where all are welcome, not a medical school where only the best and brightest can qualify. Leadership in this family is about serving, not positions or titles. The man or woman who serves is greatest. When we attempt to decree who can serve, or the extent to which they have spiritual authority, we have moved out of sync with the Spirit of Jesus, because we have reverted back to the Old Covenant way of thinking.

Becoming part of the *ecclesia* happens when a person comes to faith in Jesus, not when they believe the right doctrine or 'find their place' in a rigid top-down structure. Faith is more about belonging to a radical movement centred on Jesus than it is about believing all the right doctrines. There is a place for right belief, but that follows after faith in Christ, not necessarily before.

Jesus gave his disciples commands, and we should share those commands with people, but not in an attempt to control who can join us or to determine what role they will have in the church family.

---

[20] Matthew 8:1–22 contains several examples of Jesus' approach of abundant sowing of the gospel to find disciples that were ready to obey him. He reached out to lepers, women, scribes and centurions. When they responded he asked them to go one step further, to get in the boat with him then and there and travel to the other side of Galilee.

Jesus welcomed everyone to be part of his team: 'Are you tired? Worn out? Burned out on religion? Come to me. Get away with me and you'll recover your life. I'll show you how to take a real rest.'[21] We tend to spiritualize the invitations Jesus gave, and fail to see they were real invitations to belong to a real community of disciples.

The second question:
What is the purpose of the church?

The purpose of the church is to glorify God by loving Jesus, loving those who love Jesus, and loving those who don't know Jesus. The church exists for God and for his purposes on the earth. We do not exist for ourselves. Unless we want to stand by and watch the church become a pale, anaemic version of its God-intended self, we must discover what these three God-purposes look like practically, and then live them out with fanatic devotion. We will never find purpose for our lives apart from belonging to the subversive, revolutionary community of world-changers founded 2,000 years ago. So it's in committed community that we find purpose, for ourselves and for the church.

If you follow Jesus you are part of something greater than yourself. You were created to live for God and his glory – in the world. In fact, it is theologically accurate to say we were saved for God, not ourselves. We are justified by grace into a covenant where God is the primary partner. The goal of our salvation is not first for us, but the exaltation of the glory of God's mercy through our lives. He is the object of our salvation and we are the beneficiaries.[22] Justification by faith, therefore, is not a licence to live for ourselves but an invitation to live for God. God saves us for God's glory. It helps me to visualize it this way:

[21] Matthew 11:28, *The Message*
[22] Romans 15:7ff.

God
↓
God's Glory
↓
God's Mission
↓
God's People
↓
God's World

God started the church. And he has a mission for the church. He is on a mission to fill the whole world with his glory.[23] The church is his primary way of doing that.[24] This perspective gives us a way of valuing the little things we do every day, while keeping the big picture in mind. All of life that is lived for God is part of the mission of God. When we care for people, when we speak to them respectfully, when we participate in sports activities, when we celebrate culture and art and dance and music, and we do it with our hearts aflame for God, we give God glory. When we see ourselves as the agents of God, we are thinking holistically, and all our actions take on meaning and wonder. This sense of wonder increases when we share the reason for the hope we have with others.

The advent of postmodernism has unleashed a yearning for community, for creativity and for a cause to live and die for. My experience of pastoring an American mega-church taught me that those born after 1980 are very wary of people selling God to them. They don't want impersonal religious formulas and techniques. They don't want to sit through boring meetings watching others preach and pray. They want to be part of what is happening, up close and personal. And they don't want their experience of church to be culturally out of touch.

---

[23] Habakkuk 2:14
[24] Genesis 1:28, 12:1–3; Ephesians 3:20–21

Frost and Hirsch comment on the sad reality of purposeless church:

> The contemporary traditional church is increasingly seen as the least likely option for those seeking an artistic, politically subversive, activist community of mystical faith.[25]

The answer to the problems of purposeless Christianity is not reworking outdated and unworkable church models, but creating new wineskins and then filling them with passion for Jesus and his purposes on the earth.

Church was conceived in the heart of our Father as his way of offering forgiveness to those who are blinded by the gods of this earth and providing justice to the oppressed. We are here for God. We will not fulfil our purpose on earth by escaping from the world; we are called to invade it, not escape from it. We are here to turn dry bones of broken people into a living army of Jesus-lovers who have the life of God breathed into their being.

God planned and created the 24,000 languages and peoples of this planet, and he will not be satisfied until every one of them is filled with love for his Son, Jesus. He longs for them to be with him in heaven. There are languages on earth that have never been heard in heaven. He longs to hear his name worshipped by all the peoples of the earth before he wraps up history and brings us home. The book of Revelation paints a picture of a great party at the end of time when all nations and peoples gather around his throne and worship the Lamb of God. Father yearns for lost sons and daughters to share in the party. He wants the heavy burden of poverty and oppression lifted off them. That is why we are here.

Why I believe in 'the seamless connection'

One of the reasons the church has turned into a valley of dry bones is it has lost its apostolic passion. (More on that in a later

---

[25] Michael Frost and Alan Hirsch, *The Shaping of Things to Come*, p 6.

chapter.) There is a great chasm between the mission of God and the practices of many local churches. Nowhere is this more evident than in the great gulf between local churches and what we often refer to as 'para-church organizations'. Visionary leaders founded most of the dynamic 'para-church' ministries in the world today. Not just a few of these leaders were misunderstood by their denominations and local churches. Many of them felt they had no alternative but to leave the church they were part of to start the movement God put on their heart. Sadly, this reinforces the idea that mission and church are separate entities.

I believe deeply and fervently in the marriage of church and mission. I worked for many years in a mission agency that had little fervour for the local church. I grew increasingly uneasy about how we viewed local churches. One of my co-workers said to me at one point, 'You don't believe in "direct sending", do you?' He clarified that he believed local churches should not and could not send missionaries directly to the field, that they were not gifted or anointed by God to send people as missionaries apart from missionary organizations. That kind of thinking seems a long way from the church of Antioch in Acts 13.

On the other side of the coin, there are many local churches that have no vision for the nations and no room in their thinking or their leadership for visionary leaders that are not part of their local church. These churches are ingrown and controlling. Their god is too small and their understanding of church is too narrow.

I believe both church and mission are married in the heart of God. He holds them together. They are one in his heart. He is the chief shepherd of the church and he is the creator and redeemer of the nations. To love God passionately is to love his bride and to love his mission to a broken world. To love the nations and not be connected to others in the body of Christ is folly. To love God passionately is to love what he loves and who he loves. True passion begins with God but does not end with God. The closer we get to the heart of God in intimacy, the more we will love the church and the lost. We cannot separate them. It is a seamless connection in God's heart.

> ## *Church and mission are married in the heart of God.*

Chapters 54 and 55 of the book of Isaiah illustrate the marriage of these two truths. Isaiah 54 paints a picture of the church as a barren woman, about to have many children. Isaiah 55 gives the clearest presentation of salvation found in the Old Testament. The two chapters represent the church and God's mission to the nations.

How does the integration of these two work out practically? Let me tell you how it works for me.

I have dropped the word missionary from my vocabulary. Not because I don't believe in the mission of God, or that people should not go to the nations, but because the word missionary implies some of us are called and some are not. The truth is, we are all called.

A friend of mine in California sells insurance. He makes lots of money and wins lots of 'top salesman of the year' awards. He is really good at what he does, but his first passion is Jesus. He volunteered to go overseas. He got a passport and begged God to call him to a people who had never heard the good news about Jesus, but God told him to stay in America. Now Bill sells insurance because that is where God called him. As Bill says, 'I work full time for Jesus, I just happen to sell insurance on the side.'

No one visits Bill in his office without hearing about Jesus. Bill is a passionate lover of Jesus who was called specifically to America. Hearing a call from God is not just for those who go to other lands. We are all called to serve God full time; it is up to us to find out where that is. There are no second-class people in God's family. It is not just those who go to other lands who are called, while the rest of us just stay behind. Wouldn't that be an exciting life:

the spiritual guys get to do something exciting for God and the rest of the spiritual wusses sit around and do nothing! If God only calls people to go to other countries, that means everyone who doesn't go is a reject. Why should America or South Africa or England get all the people left behind?!

The third question: How do we do church?

Although Matthew 18:20 tells us what church is, it doesn't define how to do church. If church in its simplest form is a few people gathering in his name, and the purpose of the church is to glorify God by loving Jesus, loving each other and loving those who don't know Jesus, that still doesn't answer some of the practical questions about how church functions. Yes, we are to love each other. But what does that mean? How do we do that practically?

We learn the answer to that question in Acts 2:41–47. This passage of Scripture is not just good history. It is in the Bible to give us a model, an example of how the church grows into spiritual maturity. As you read through this passage (quoted below from *The Message*), I suggest you take out a pen and underline the activities done in the early church that you think might result in healthy spiritual growth for your church community:

> That day about three thousand took him at his word, were baptized and were signed up. They committed themselves to the teaching of the apostles, the life together, the common meal, and the prayers. Everyone around was in awe—all those wonders and signs done through the apostles! And all the believers lived in a wonderful harmony, holding everything in common. They sold whatever they owned and pooled their resources so that each person's need was met. They followed a daily discipline of worship in the Temple followed by meals at home, every meal a celebration, exuberant and joyful, as they praised God. People in general liked what they saw. Every day their number grew as God added those who were saved.

What activities did you underline? Here are the ones I highlighted:

1. Telling people about Jesus – they 'took him at his word' as Peter preached to the crowds about Jesus – verse 41
2. Water baptism – verse 41
3. Teaching the Bible – 'apostles' doctrine' – verse 42
4. Hanging out, building community – 'the life together' – verse 42
5. Communion – 'the common meal' – verse 42
6. Sharing meals together – 'every meal a celebration' – verse 46
7. Prayer – verse 42
8. Giving to one another and to the work of ministry – verse 45
9. Meeting in small groups from house to house and in large celebrations in the Temple – verse 46
10. Worship – 'they praised God' – verse 47
11. Multiplication – 'their number grew as God added those who were being saved' – verse 47

I group all these activities into three categories:

○ The *upward aspect* of church has to do with worship, communion, daily disciplines of prayer and gathering with other communities for celebration (see numbers 5, 7, 9 and 10 above).
○ The *inward aspect* of church is about giving to each other, eating meals together, playing and hanging out together, mentoring one another, meeting in men's and women's Bible study groups and accountability times, and studying the word together (numbers 2, 3, 4, 5, 8, and 9 above).
○ The *outward and forward* aspect of church is telling people about Jesus, baptizing new Christians and reproducing churches in other locations (1, 2, 8, and 11 above).

What does simple church look like in action?

Church is as simple as gathering around a meal, laughing and fellowshipping together. It should regularly include breaking bread and remembering the Lord's death, preferably around meals and times of fellowship, singing and praying, laying hands on those in need, and giving to each other and to the ministries of the community as it reaches out to others. It can be as practical as asking the Lord: 'How can we reach out to our friends and neighbours together?' then obeying what he tells us to do. These are not just nice words: I really believe we should pray and listen often to what God would have us do, share our impressions, then get up and do it! You will be amazed at the results!

Simple church includes celebration in large gatherings whenever possible, but not as a focus of how we do church. Simple church doesn't always mean small church. There is a place for large meetings. They inspire people to remember they are part of something bigger than themselves. Large celebrations inspire faith and point the way forward for the whole congregation or network of churches. Ideally, celebrations occur when a 'church of churches' comes together. I suggest that that should not happen more than once a month, lest the focus be diverted from the simplicity of church life to the big event.

Vision from God for church in its simplest form is a powerful thing. Church is people, ordinary people, living their lives for Jesus. No hype, not mad at anyone, no special revelation or new doctrine or wonder-leader, just friends obeying Jesus together. Do you want to be part of a church community that is relationally and intentionally reaching out to other people? That is simple church.

God will give you a fresh vision for the simplicity of church if you ask him. But be careful, if you ask for it, God will give it to you and it will be like a burning fire in you that takes over your life!

Vision precedes reality. If you want a vision of how God sees the church, ask God to let you see what he sees and feel what he feels. That is what happened to the prophet Ezekiel: God showed him a valley of dry bones. But God saw an army.[26] God opened Ezekiel's eyes and he saw the valley of dry bones from God's perspective. Seeing the ancient vision of Ezekiel for yourself means you start dreaming about how church can be. It will give you something powerful to hold onto when you bump up against the politics of institutional church, or are used by people in the name of God. A vision from God is simply a God-given way of seeing things as he sees them. It's a picture of what he wants for your life, and no one can take that from you. A person with a vision is not a prisoner of a person without one. More importantly, you will not be the prisoner of super-Christians who try to one-up everyone with the latest and greatest experience or revelation or vision.

> *A person with a vision is not a prisoner of a person without one.*

Vision from God burning in your heart will challenge the status quo in your life. It will enable you to break free from your dependency on programmes and buildings that offend you or make you feel okay about yourself. It will challenge past ways of doing things so you can dream new dreams. Every person needs a vision of the church from God's perspective. Every person who is hungry to grow in God needs a vision from God for his or her part in the church, the *ecclesia*. A fresh vision of church in its simplicity will create courage in your heart to break from the old and try the new. It will inspire you and your friends to resist the temptations to cynicism and give you courage to act on your beliefs. Vision from God for his church will give you faith for the church you are

---

[26] Ezekiel 37

part of. You will see how much God loves the church. You will pray for her and weep for her, and if necessary, leave her. You will be free to love, forgive and submit to her and her leaders as well – if that is what God says to do.

When God imparts a vision, and he finds someone with courage to take hold of that vision and run with it, God himself will stand behind it. If he gave it, it is *his* vision. He will complete what he starts in you, as long you obey him and act with integrity and humility. Even if you make mistakes, God will rescue you if you ask for his mercy. No force on earth or demon in hell can keep you from the *will of God*, if you walk obediently before God and humbly before others.

> *No force on earth or demon in hell can keep you from the will of God, if you walk obediently before God and humbly before others.*

When people receive and act on a vision given by God, God will get behind them. Great things happen in the ordinary parts of our lives when we obey God. It won't be easy, but your journey will be with God. What more could you ask than to go on a journey with the Creator? There are many stories of others who have gone on this same journey, and found fresh life and hope. Pete Greig tells the story of how God gave him 'The Vision' in *Red Moon Rising*. He wrote down the words on the wall of a prayer room, and a world-wide prayer movement was born. Now thousands of young people in over 50 nations are discovering a new way of doing church as they connect in prayer rooms and committed communities called 'boiler rooms'.[27]

Pete followed his dream for his generation. Will you follow

---

[27] For more on this see Pete Greig and Dave Roberts, *Red Moon Rising,* Survivor 2004; and Andy Freeman and Pete Greig, *PunkMonk,* Survivor 2007.

your dream of church for this season in your life? For your generation? For your nation and your people?

Well done, good and famous servant

It's not just the famous who lead the church. God's army does not
march single file behind a few famous people. It is made up of a
vast multitude of hidden people, people who are doing church
and want nothing more than to live what they read about in the
book of Acts. Many are doing great exploits for God that no one
ever hears about. It's this 'army of the ordinary' that I want to be
part of. Without exaggeration, there are several hundred million
followers of Jesus living in countries that are closed to Christianity who have no building to meet in, no pastor, no one with a formal education to lead the children's ministry or singles
programme nor anyone to entertain the youth on Wednesday
nights. All they have is Jesus and a few people that meet secretly
in the woods or quietly in someone's home.

My wife, Sally, and I are part of a simple church. As I write this,
there are three couples and two singles. We share meals together,
walk the streets of townships together, and disciple one another
and spur each other on to multiply simple churches among the
people we are reaching out to. We have a vision for a network of
scores of simple churches meeting on every street, in every school
and shop and restaurant and car-park! Why not dream a big
dream?

In our work with All Nations, Sally and I get to work beside
some amazing people serving in very strange and fascinating
places. Like Pam. Pam served for quite a few years in a closed
country in Asia.[28] Pam was a young woman when God challenged

---

[28] There are many countries that do not grant 'missionary visas' but who will give
visas to people if they add value to the country through creating employment or serving the practical needs of their people.

her to go. Her pastor blessed her but told her they wouldn't be able to send her out, which meant she would need to find other people to back her financially.

Pam was one of the first outside people to learn the language of the people she went to in Asia. She has come up with innovative ideas for telling people about Jesus, ideas that others mocked when they heard about them. But her ideas worked. They worked because God inspired them. Pam prayed, God gave her an idea, and as a result people have come to Jesus and simple churches have been started. Pam is one of my heroes. She is not famous, but she has been faithful.

Matt and Elizabeth Chen serve on the international leadership team of All Nations. The Chens started out in a small Bible study group over 15 years ago. Today, hundreds of people have come to Christ from Buddhist backgrounds through their efforts. Eighty-five per cent of the people in their church are first-generation followers of Jesus. The Chens oversee a church-planting movement that is in its infant stages, but is growing and sure to impact many thousands of people. Living Water, the church they pastor, is sending out workers to start more churches in other cities and countries in Asia.

> *Eighty-five per cent of the people in their church are first-generation followers of Jesus.*

It wasn't always a time of such blessing for the Chens. Matt sat for years in a mega-church without being recognized or called out. He learned English and endured years of communicating in a second language, often overlooked or misunderstood. But God saw Matt's heart and he anointed Matt with an apostolic calling to plant churches and raise up others to do the same. Matt was not famous, but he was faithful. Someday he will hear God say 'well done'. You know why? Matt stepped out in faith. God gave him a vision of doing church in people's homes, and he started empowering and releasing people. He felt a stirring in his heart, paid attention to God's stirring, and God blessed him.

Movements of simple churches

There are spontaneous movements of simple churches taking place all over the world. If you want to get a bigger picture of what God is doing through these movements, read David Garrison's book, *Church Planting Movements*,[29] or Wolfgang Simson's challenging and inspiring view of church in *Houses That Change the World*.[30] Garrison tells stories of movements taking place in South America, Cambodia, China, India and other parts of the globe. He describes the common characteristics of these movements. It is their simplicity that makes them so powerful: home-based (not based in 'church' buildings), small, Bible-oriented, outreach-focused, led by non-professionals, enjoying passionate prayer and worship, grass roots, and quick to reproduce.

I am part of one of these movements. It's not because I'm in love with a 'model' of church. Nor am I in love with church planting per se. But I am in love with Jesus and his church. I love every part of his church. But having said that, I am most passionate about doing church in a way that makes it possible for those who have never heard the good news to be part of the church. The ministry I lead is actually a network of churches and partner churches, all of which are passionate about church-planting movements where people don't know Jesus. We are not concerned about the brand on the door but the people on the street. The latest research reveals that 3.3 billion people have never heard the name of Jesus one time. There are 5,750 people groups that have no church-planting activity among them. I love simple

---

[29] David Garrison, *Church Planting Movements*, WIGTake Resources 2003.

[30] Wolfgang Simson, *Houses That Change the World*, Paternoster 2001.

church because it makes church accessible to the greatest number of people. It doesn't require a professional or a building or a charismatic personality to lead a simple church.

All Nations provides training for those interested in this approach to church planting through a short, hands-on learning experience we call CPx (Church Planting Xperience).[31] Interestingly, we have to train people from traditional and institutional church backgrounds out of the old way of doing church, and orient them to the new paradigm of simple church. It is this way of doing church that makes it possible for Buddhists, Muslims, and Hindus – and increasingly, postmodern Western youth – to experience church like we read about in the book of Acts. I jokingly say to those we train, 'You never have to worry about losing your job . . . because you will never have one.' In other words, the key to passing the torch to the next generation of leaders in simple-church-planting movements is never to hold the torch, speaking of positions and titles. We teach people to be a servant leader who raises up others to carry the torch from the beginning. This is a new style of leadership that requires serving behind the scenes, being secure enough to be a coach to new leaders without position or title. The goal of a simple-church-planting movement is not being an up-front pastor or elder, but being a spiritual father or mother to a movement of elders and church planters.

Those who lead in such a movement need to be secure enough not to have a title like pastor or elder. The idea is to help people know Jesus personally, mentor them, and then encourage them to gather their friends and form a small, simple church. When that happens, the church planter is really serving as an influencer behind the scenes to mentor and coach new leaders. What hinders the spontaneous multiplication that takes place naturally in such movements is a Western, institutional church model of leadership. By staying in the background and mentoring and

---

[31] Contact www.all-nations.info or www.floydandsally.org for more information.

coaching others, especially those who have the potential to lead, servant-hearted leaders lay the foundation for a spontaneous movement of churches to be born. There is still spiritual authority being exercised, but it is authority based on relationship. It is apostolic not hierarchical.

The church is like a beautiful woman in a beauty contest

I have lived with a vision of God revealing himself through the church since the church became more than a bad word to me. God gave me a picture of what a dry-bones army of people can be for him, and that picture has captured me since that time. God is busy revealing himself to the world, through the church. Not through institutions or programmes or buildings, but through simple, ordinary people, people willing to give up their broken lives in exchange for his life lived through them.

The church reveals the beauty of God

A beauty contest happened right before the eyes of the people in Jerusalem, and the church won the contest, hands down. God showed off his beauty through ordinary people. It was actually not much of a contest. The religion of the scribes and Pharisees didn't stand a chance. All the followers of Jesus needed to do was love each other. By living the way they did, they displayed Jesus before people who were hungry for reality. They allowed Jesus to be seen through them as they shared their food with the poor, treated women as equals, and empowered every member to do their part in leading and serving. People saw compassion in action as the disciples prayed for the sick and ate and laughed and cried together. God used them to breathe life on bones, and those bones got up and walked.

A beauty contest happened right before the eyes of the people in Jerusalem, and the church won the contest, hands down. God showed off his beauty through ordinary people.

As Sally and I and our team in Cape Town are getting involved with people in the poorer communities of the city, we are coming into contact with some of the most broken people imaginable. I think there is not a human problem we aren't encountering. But we love the people God has called us to. We don't see them by the colour of their skin or their level of poverty. We see their potential. We see the broken people we feed and clothe and house with eyes of faith. We see what God can do through them. We often talk about the new life our small band of disciples have in Jesus. It doesn't make any difference to us that most of them have no idea of their own potential. The important thing is that we know it is true, that Father loves them and has put that love in our hearts for them. We know he loves them, we know their potential, so we tell them. And you know what? They believe us!

I feel the same way about simple church today. When I share my passion for God's glory being revealed through the church, some people have no idea what I'm talking about. The vision is hidden from them in plain sight. It's right there in the book of Acts. It's all over Paul's letters. It's being lived out in radical communities all around us. But I have learned that a man with a vision is not the prisoner of people without one. I realize that God has to get people to a place of 'holy frustration' before they are ready to learn about church the way he wants to do it. I know what his word says. I know the church is beautiful in his eyes. I know his heart for simple church, so I carry his vision whether people see it or not. I am filled with hope!

The church reveals the glory of God

The church is God's idea. He started it and he leads it. The church is God's way of showing off his incredible glory through transformed lives. This glory lived out in simple-church communities is God's evidence to a godless world that he is real. Jesus prayed for it to happen:

> The same glory you gave me, I gave them,
> So they'll be as unified and together as we are —
> I in them and you in me.
> Then they'll be mature in this oneness
> And give the godless world evidence
> That you've sent me and loved them
> In the same way you've loved me.[32]

The people we work with, the poor and unemployed Muslims, people who have suffered sexual abuse, and those suffering from life-controlling addictions, are not the exception in life, but the norm. In the past I naïvely thought the rest of the Christians in the world were a lot better off than the people we are reaching out to. But after more than 40 years of serving Jesus in many different countries, I am convinced the brokenness and pain we encounter in the lives of people in Cape Town is the same brokenness we encounter in ordinary people everywhere.

For the busy executive and the hustling drug dealer on the streets, the behaviour may be different but the pain is the same. Some people are alcoholics, others are workaholics. Some folks are prisoners of fear, some are performing hard to drive away their fears. A few people use hard drugs, others find different kinds of drugs. Everyone dulls the pain somehow. We all suffer from one degree of brokenness or another. Dysfunctional parents, abandonment or abuse all work their terrible price on each

---

[32] John 17:22–23, *The Message*

of us. Everyone carries the marks of imperfect parents or being raised without a father who knew how to express his love.

We all suffer from one degree of brokenness or another.

In contrast to what our team is doing in Cape Town, listen to how Bill Hybels shares his experience of working closely with the 'powerful' from his many visits to Washington, DC:

> For eight years during the decade of the nineties I went to Washington, DC every month to meet in the foremost centers of power with some of the highest elected officials in our country. What I discovered was not how powerful those people are, but how limited their power really is. All they can actually do is rearrange the yard markers on the playing field of life. They can't change a human heart. They can't heal a wounded soul. They can't turn hatred into love. . .[33]

Into this powerless, bruised and hurting world, God not only sent a Saviour, he raised up the church to be a constant source of the Saviour's presence. You are that church! The church stewards the grace and love of God on earth. That is the glory of God. God lives in us. Weak as we are, he has chosen to dwell in us. We are where the glory of God is found. Not primarily in great conferences and well-run programmes and institutions of the church, but in the ordinary men and women who make up the church.

The church reveals the love of God

I received the bad news while I was away on a speaking trip. I came home to a very distraught family who lost their little one-week-old son, Isaac. The first time I saw the parents after returning was at the graveside service. Though the sadness was palpable, one message came through loud and clear: Ray and

---

[33] Bill Hybels, *Courageous Leadership*, Zondervan 2002, p 21.

Maxine Nelson and their little daughter, Briana, had been surrounded by friends from their home group who loved them. They
sat with them at the hospital, brought them meals, and cried with
them in their pain and confusion. The Nelsons' parents, who had
flown in from out of state and from another country, couldn't
believe all the love being poured out on their children. Ray Nelson took me aside after the graveside service and said, 'We feel
really taken care of by our friends. John and Patty and Amy and
our home group have been amazing. They were with us in the
hospital when Isaac was delivered. They prayed with us and
believed God was with us when we asked him to spare Isaac's life.
They helped us when it seemed so hard we couldn't take the pain
and disappointment. They brought us meals and "loved on" our
hearts. We have been surrounded with love.'

I thought afterwards: what would the Nelsons have done without a community of friends to love them through this painful
time? How hard would it have been for them without friends to
share their sorrows and help them move forward after family and
relatives went back home? Simple church is people loving people.
They show the love of God. God cares for his people through
other people. The church reveals the love of God when we stand
with each other, especially when there are no pat answers or easy
solutions.

Though it doesn't happen this way every time, the Nelsons had
another baby boy a year later. This time he was a healthy, happy
boy, born one year to the day after their first son died!

The church is God's way of inviting us to live for something far
greater than ourselves. His love awakens desire in our hearts as
we grow with others in community. It is not an easy journey, but
it is God's way of teaching us to love. Our hearts come alive as we
are cared for and loved and forgiven and restored, and as we do
the same for others. We discover who we are as the children of
God through loving relationships. This is the purpose of God for
the church, to love as Jesus would if he were walking around in

our bodies. In fact, he is walking the earth today, in us. We are Jesus to people who don't know him.

The church is God's way of building bridges between those of different races and colours. The church heals those in pain and opens its arms to those without hope. The church speaks for God in times of crisis, and calms the fearful when they are overwhelmed with life's cares. The church is there in times of tragedy and grieving. It helps break the chains of addictions and speaks truth to the confused. The church is God's prophetic voice in the face of injustice. Whatever the problem, whatever the need, God has placed within the church the resources necessary to respond. The empowering presence of God dwells in the church. And it is there, in the family of the redeemed, that we discover our part in the purposes of God.

Don't forget who you are

Several years ago, my daughter Misha had a frightening experience that temporarily robbed her of her memory. She suffered an amniotic fluid embolism while giving birth to her second child, Luke. Without warning, as she was about to give birth, her lungs filled with fluid and she passed out. The doctors rushed her into surgery and delivered the baby c-section. Misha was without oxygen for up to 14 minutes while a team of 12 doctors and nurses worked on her feverishly to revive her heart and stop the clotting and haemorrhaging taking place simultaneously in her blood. It was a medical crisis of the worst kind for a birthing mother.

Misha lived due to the wonderful care of her physicians and the intervention of God. The doctors were very concerned about lasting harm to Misha. Most mothers who survive this type of crisis are brain damaged by the loss of oxygen. Misha was especially disoriented the first few days after her surgery. We were greatly concerned about lasting effects on her memory or personality or the ability to be a mother and wife for her family.

In the first few days when we visited Misha in the ICU, she wasn't sure where she was or what had happened to her. After a few days it became obvious that her personality was totally the same as the vibrant, outgoing girl she had always been. But she forgot most things we talked about from one day to the next. We had humorous moments teasing Misha about what she said, but all of us were deeply concerned that she would experience serious memory loss. We didn't want her to forget who she was, her family, and the wonderful promises God had given her for her life.

In the weeks following the crisis, it became obvious that Misha was totally healed. Though she had no recollection of the tragic events surrounding her surgery, she completely recovered. The doctors have assured Misha that her case will go down in medical history. Her doctor cried every time Misha came in for her check-ups. She told her that she just couldn't believe how normal and happy she was. Both she and her baby are well and have no lasting effects from what happened to them. Amazingly, her memory is totally restored. It happened with the help of her husband, Lionel, who rehearsed with Misha what happened to her. He helped her remember important events leading up to the birth, and soon the memories came flooding back.

In the same way, God has placed us in his family and surrounded us with brothers and sisters to remind us of who we are and the destiny we have as the family of God. Don't forget who you are! He doesn't want you to experience memory loss, short term or long term, concerning who you are or why you are here on earth. God wants us to know and remember our identity and destiny. If we forget, God the Father loves to remind us that he has a plan and destiny for our lives. He places us in families and unfolds our destiny for us as we turn our lives over to him.

PART TWO
Courageous Leadership

3

Courage to Change

God designed and created the church to organize itself

Parents around the world manage to have children and provide for them without books or university degrees. Fathers and mothers have figured out for centuries how to lead and organize their families. It's written into our DNA as parents. Sure, we should learn to be better mothers and fathers through good mentoring and teaching, but the basic ingredients are in us. God designed us to love and care for our own. It is natural to how he made us.

God puts within all creation innate laws of self-perpetuation and self-governance. I love the outdoors. I try to take a few days each year to get away from work and people, and spend as much time as possible in the 'bush' as it is called in Africa. I enjoy watching wild animals. The silent kudu, the majestic gemsbok, and the strange-looking wildebeest all have their own unique ways. Wild animals intuitively know when it will rain, how to stay downwind of their natural enemies, and how to guard their young. Not being a big fan of zoos, I have noticed that wild animals do quite well at taking care of themselves without zookeepers to lock them up and feed them.

The same principles apply to simple church. Too much structure, or the wrong kind of leadership, hinders simple churches from functioning and multiplying the way God designed them to. The very things that make conventional mega-churches successful will hinder the growth and spontaneous expansion of simple churches. The churches Paul planted were simple in nature. Paul patiently waited to appoint leaders in the churches he started until they had time to grow and find their way. Sometimes he left them to develop on their own, encouraging them to build on the values, truths and passions he imparted to them while he was with them. He trusted the Holy Spirit in them to guide them. When Paul returned to the churches he'd planted after some months, or a year or two on, he recognized and set in place elders to lead the network of simple home-based churches they had become.

There is a time and place to train spiritual leaders. But if we get ahead of God's timetable in people's lives, it may actually hinder natural development. If we try to force growth in spiritual leaders before they are ready, it creates problems, such as a performance mentality, unhealthy dependency, and an inability to think and discern for oneself. Paul wrote to Timothy and gave him guidelines for selecting and appointing elders in the church in Ephesus, but this was in a church that had been functioning for years. Those guidelines were descriptive of healthy leadership, not prescriptive. Establishing rules for how things should be done often hinders growth more than helping it.

God has placed all the gifts and ministries that were in Jesus in the church, and more importantly, Jesus himself lives within the church. We don't need leadership hierarchies, quality-control systems, and other man-made mechanisms to make us function properly. We do need fathers and mothers to care for us, and truth to guide us. We don't need overseers who smother or control us.

A few years ago I visited the team leader of a spontaneously reproducing simple-church movement in Central India called Din Bandu. I sat with the leader of this movement, along with the village workers who travelled and preached the good news. Over 7,000 newly baptized Hindus had come to Christ through these brothers and sisters. I was deeply impacted by the humility of these men and women. Most of them had been stoned, beaten or imprisoned for their faith.

I asked the team leader what he thought would be the greatest hindrance to the continued growth of the movement. He replied, 'Western models of church government.' When I asked what he meant, he said that the churches in their movement organized naturally around those who went from village to village, preaching and baptizing. Leaders in the movement were those who led people to Christ. The ones doing the baptizing were the village workers and their mentors. The churches that were started were connected organically, as the believers told others about their new faith, moving from village to village – just as families are connected through cousins, nephews, aunts and uncles. This leader saw that his primary role was to recognize those who were already doing the work of ministry, select them for further training, and assist them as the movement grew.

As I watched him equip his leaders, it occurred to me that there is a beautiful sense of design and order built into the spiritual DNA of the church of Jesus Christ. The role of leaders is to affirm and serve this design, not impose structures on top of it. Those who appreciate the beauty and innate order of God's natural design for the church serve the church with the greatest wisdom.

What gives the church cohesion in such a model? Its values and vision. When the values and vision of the kingdom are clearly understood by those who father and mother a movement, and they are clearly articulated for all to understand, and imparted through discipling relationships, the DNA of the movement takes hold in people's hearts.

To the degree people in a movement of simple churches hold their values and vision in common, the movement does not need top-down 'command-and-control' church government. Those in the movement know how to live because they believe the values and are passionate about the vision. They don't need to be told what to do or how to live. That is the difference between a spontaneously reproducing movement and a group of churches that are reproduced cookie-cutter fashion, one at a time. The franchise model of church multiplication must have a command-and-control structure of church government to hold everyone accountable to its beliefs. A man or woman has to be in charge at the top. But a spontaneous, out-of-control, book-of-Acts-type movement has a different make-up altogether. It organizes around the life of Christ in the people, around what the Spirit is doing through the people, and the word of God as it takes root in the hearts of the people.

The question I have wrestled with for the last 20 years in this regard is, how do you nurture a movement to multiply spontaneously, and at the same time provide apostolic leadership? In other words, how do you live out the New Testament principles of church government and not stifle what the Holy Spirit is doing? I have tried different approaches to find the right balance, and have failed to get it right most of the time. But as I learn from my mistakes, I am more convinced than ever that we can have biblical order and still be an out-of-human-control, church-multiplying movement. There was order in the midst of the chaos of the early church. The apostles and elders played vital roles in keeping focused in growing in the right direction, and that inspires me to believe the same can happen today.

Neil Cole says it well when addressing this issue:

> Just as in nature, DNA in the church provides the intrinsic code necessary for control, order and form. We must have more faith in Christ's DNA – divine truth, nurturing relationships, and apostolic mission – than in our own human structures and controls . . . Structures are needed, but they must be simple, reproducible, and internal rather than external. Every living thing is made up of structure and

systems . . . The universe and nature itself teach us that order is possible even when there is no control but God Himself.[1]

If we are to change the way we do church, there must be a vision of something greater happening through our churches than what is going on at present. Our present forms of church government are perfectly suited to produce the results we are now seeing – that is the problem! How we typically lead and organize churches is built on a model of maintenance and direction, not geared for spontaneous expansion. We have learned how to control the church, but we struggle to learn how to allow the Holy Spirit to be in control.

> Our present forms of church government are perfectly suited to produce the results we are now seeing - that is the problem!

The kind of leadership that is needed in church-planting movements should not be highly visible. It is leadership that follows what is happening, not tries to be in control of what happens. Because we are Sunday-meeting focused, instead of everyday-movement focused, we immediately think about how disorderly our church meetings will become if there is no order. But think bigger: if our churches are growing spontaneously, our problems will change. Our focus will not be about meetings alone, as important as they are, but how to disciple the leaders as they disciple new converts and equip leaders to lead and reproduce themselves.

Western models of management have tended to dominate how we do church: reporting relationships, span of control, job descriptions, quality control, budgets, flow charts, and so on. But the way the church organized itself in the books of Acts was

---

[1] Neil Cole, *Organic Church*, p 124.

different. Though there was recognized authority in the men and women Jesus called to lead the movement he founded, it was not a top-down authority. It flowed along a flat line of relationships and reproduction. Where there was no natural relationship with new converts, and where there were no new churches to serve, there was no need for 'positional' authority over those churches. The way of the church by its divine design is decentralized expansion, whereas the way of the flesh is to control and command what happens.

Simple-church movements can function with invisible structures, like water pipes in a home. The pipes are important, but we don't sit around and brag about people's water pipes. It is the water and how it tastes that counts.[2] Pipes serve a function. Some pipes are bigger than others, but they exist to bring us water. Water pipes are only as important as the water they bring to us. So it is with church government. Structure should only be created where it meets a need. Structures should not be created where there is no life. When people are coming to Christ regularly, when the community is growing spontaneously, when you have to make decisions about growth problems, then you need some structure, but only what is necessary for the moment. Always strive to keep it simple and invisible, and then you will be safe.

Structure should never control life, only serve it. Only involve people in structures who are secure with being out of sight and serving. You don't use a water hose to build water pipes in a large block of flats, nor should you invite someone to be an elder who doesn't have water flowing through them to the lost, or only a small flow of life. Elders are people who 'eld', who do the stuff of ministry outside the flock as well as inside. If they have the values and live the vision, they are already bringing water to the thirsty.

The command-and-control leadership structure, which most

---

[2] Adapted from Neil Cole, *Organic Church*, p 126.

churches borrow from the Western management models, looks like this:

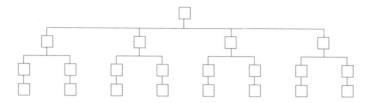

In contrast, an organic flow chart for a simple-church movement looks like this:

Again and again I am asked when I teach on this subject, 'How can there be quality control in a simple-church movement?' (By 'quality control' people typically mean, 'How can we guarantee the churches will not fall into heresy?') I point out that having a top-down command-and-control structure does not guarantee right doctrine, morality among leaders, and certainly does not mean quality of life and growth of new believers. All we have to do is look at top-down, command-and-control denominations to realize this is true.

It's about bonding and first impressions

Years ago I learned about the principle of bonding or imprinting.[3] This is a process whereby a newly hatched baby duckling or baby

---

[3] I learned this concept from Tom and Betty Sue Brewster, who use a language-learning approach based on bonding to people in one's host culture.

chick becomes bonded to the first moving object on which the hatchling focuses its eyes. That becomes the mother, even if it happens to be a dog or a human being. God designed us as humans to function this way as well. This is so we would form a strong bond between our mother and ourselves. That is why a new-born human baby will often 'bond' to a nursing sister instead of the birth mother if the mother is not the first one to hold the baby. The baby is quiet while the sister holds the baby, then starts crying when it is given to Mum. Unfortunately, the baby has had time to bond to the wrong person.

In our work of training cross-cultural church planters, we learned that there is a tendency for new missionaries in a foreign field to be met at the airport and then whisked off to the mission-ary compound. The old-timers want to show hospitality, protect the newcomers from making mistakes, and ease them into their new culture. But this is a huge mistake. The new workers don't 'bond' to their host culture or the people they are called to reach, but to other missionaries!

Neil Cole tells about the film *Fly Away Home* in his book *Organic Church*. A young girl finds a nest of hatchlings, and they bond to her as their mother. At first, this is a lot of fun. The girl finds loyal companions, and the baby geese find that the girl meets their needs. Wherever she goes she is followed by a gag-gle of young geese expecting her to feed them, protect them and train them how to be good geese. As much as the young girl loves them, the question that emerges is, 'How can she teach them to fly in formation and to head south for the winter?' Their survival depends on her example. In the film her dad finds a way for her to do that, but it is a lot of work and totally unnatural.

The challenge in church today is that people are 'imprinted' by other people who don't have the DNA of radical New Testament church. They have bonded to meeting-oriented church, to church done for them by pastors, and to church that is conducted in a building one day a week. They have a DNA of dependency on the life-support systems of Sunday school, youth programmes and men's and women's ministries. I often picture this kind of church as a very sick patient in an ICU ward, in isolation, hooked up to life-support systems. And that is what conventional church does for many people: they are dependent on the ministries of the church. Church for these people is not a radical movement where they are leading people to Christ and baptizing their converts weekly, but something that exists to serve them, to keep them alive.

> *If their leaders don't reproduce followers of Jesus, the people won't believe it is a high value in the church.*

If the leaders and members of conventional churches are busy maintaining the business systems and structures of the church, and don't have time to be winning people to Christ, the people will bond to the Western business-oriented DNA of their leaders. If their leaders don't reproduce followers of Jesus, the people won't believe it is a high value in the church. If the leaders see themselves as the ones who run the church instead of those who preach to the lost and disciple new believers, then the people will be imprinted with that DNA. The DNA of a church at the deepest level sets the pattern of who the church becomes. It is that pattern that determines how everything else grows and reproduces, or doesn't grow at all.

People do what they see their leaders do

When I read about the church in the book of Acts, the leaders were in marketplaces preaching, not in board meetings deciding how to spend the tithes and offerings. They appointed others to take care of those matters. They lived the DNA they wanted to pass on. They were deliberate about what they taught and imparted. They had caught the DNA from Jesus and they wanted others to catch it from Jesus as well, breathing life through them. His life and methods were imprinted on them, and they in turn imprinted others. That is how God raises up dry bones and breathes life into them.

That is why Paul produced churches that spontaneously reproduced churches. He confidently told those he led to Christ:

> You received the message with joy from the Holy Spirit in spite of the severe suffering it brought you . . . you imitated both us and the Lord. As a result, you yourselves became an example to all the Christians in Greece . . . now the word of the Lord is ringing out from you to people everywhere, even beyond Greece, for wherever we go we find people telling us about your faith in God.[4]

You imitated me and, as a result, you became an example to all the Christians in Greece, and to people everywhere! That is DNA replication. It is what leadership is all about: reproducing the life of Christ in us in others. Because it is reproducing the life of Christ, we directly connect people to Jesus as the head of the church. The church that has this kind of leader will maintain better quality than through management-controls or top-down leadership structures.

Shared authority, not top-down authority

Sally and I were part of the Jesus movement in the 1970s. *Time* magazine wrote an article about the worldwide nature of the movement and described our work in Afghanistan and on the hippy trail. We were pretty impressed with ourselves for making the pages of *Time*, but really all you had to do in those days to see people come to Christ was show up and tell people about Jesus! The Holy Spirit was moving all over the world. Those we led to Christ, from Morocco to Marseilles, started one simple-

---

[4] 1 Thessalonians 1:6–8, NLT

church community after another, spread out in some 15 different countries. It was an exciting time and I learned tons about the church and leadership in the church.

We saw church as community, and believed we were to function like the church in the book of Acts. We fasted and prayed, met each morning for prayer, and lived simple lives of devotion to Jesus. Leadership in a simple-church movement like ours worked best when we did not try to prescribe how things were to be done, but simply kept pointing our co-workers to the book of Acts. We often 'organized' outreaches by simply encouraging people to pray and ask the Holy Spirit where they were to go that day. We even coined a phrase for what we did. We called it 'wandering in the Spirit'. We could describe it and impart it but we weren't able to prescribe it. Things were happening too quickly for us to do that.

We were too oriented to reaching the hippy culture of our day to function in a top-down, hierarchical structure. And besides, we were spread too far apart for that to work. We had communities everywhere from London to Auckland, and Goa to San Jose. We had a few core values, we shared them diligently, and trusted Jesus in our converts. We taught our disciples to do what the Holy Spirit told them to do. We had a very simple approach: live in simple community, share Jesus with everyone we could, meet people's needs, disciple one another, and start more communities. We sent those who were new believers to start new communities after six months. They did and they grew because they had to depend on Jesus. We were smart enough to know we needed the assistance of godly mothers and fathers, so we stayed close to mature believers to counsel us – *as we kept winning and reproducing more disciples for Jesus.*

Our converts were our workers

Our converts were our workers. They did much better than the recruits we tried to mobilize from Bible colleges and youth groups in the West. They had too many ideas and too many needs tied to how church was done back home.

After a person was baptized and had followed Jesus for a few months, we invited them to join what we called our workers' meetings. They were part of the team that took responsibility for what happened. We made the major decisions together. I understood and believed in leaders leading, but I also felt it was important to share the responsibility and authority as much as possible.

I look back now and see how vital our approach was to the growth of our converts. They responded to the approach we took of sharing the load. By inviting them to be part of the 'inner workings' of how things were done, they took ownership and grew quickly. I maintained the responsibility to make final decisions in case of a dispute, but only exercised that authority a few times in as many years. I taught the New Testament principles of eldership, and described what we were doing as what the elders did in the book of Acts. We didn't use that term, but we operated by those principles.

I described what we were doing as 'shared authority' not 'surrendered authority'. I led, but I adjusted my style of leadership and my approach to leadership so we could work as a team. It happened naturally as we functioned as a simple Jesus community committed to reaching out to others. I recognized then as I do now that all authority comes from God. I also taught that authority has to be earned by the character of a person who leads. I believed that true authority had to be recognized and granted from those who follow.

I describe a little later in this chapter the different kinds of authority written about in the New Testament. I think it is important to say that many leaders misunderstand what Jesus said about being a servant. When correcting his disciples because of their aspirations for position and recognition in his kingdom, Jesus said,

'I have no right to say who will sit on the thrones next to mine. God has prepared those places for the ones he has chosen.' When the ten other disciples discovered what James and John had asked, they were indignant. So Jesus called them together and said, 'You know that in this world kings are tyrants, and officials lord it over the people beneath them. But among you it should be quite different. Whoever wants to be a leader among you must be your servant.'[5]

Like Jesus, we don't have the right to say who can and cannot do things for God. We cannot set limits on people's spiritual authority.

Many leaders get this backwards. They teach that if you have a position in the kingdom of God it is important to lead as a servant. But Jesus meant us to see that those who first serve are indeed the leaders others will follow. Position and title are useless in such an arrangement. Jesus is our example. No title, no position, no place in the hierarchy of the Jewish governmental structure. This represents a radical change in how we do church – and it will take great courage to teach and model this way of leading. It is risky, but it is worth the risk. But it won't mix with conventional church models.

In a flat structure like we had in our ministry in Afghanistan, authority was delegated – not from layers of leadership above us, but from Jesus and those of us who earned the right to lead by serving others in our community, myself included. God distributes authority in simple-church communities to each person. People who lead do so without needing permission or position to get on with carrying out the great commission. One's 'covering' is found in his or her position in Christ, and not in human positions above them in the chain of command. There is a place to recognize leaders, but it flows out of who we are in Christ. It comes from heart-level humility that others recognize and accept.

The dangers of the top-down hierarchical model of command-and-control-type leadership is that it ties people to a chain of command, and creates dependency on other people for empowerment

5 Mark 10:40–43, NLT

and permission to minister. A codependency is developed that is unhealthy and will not lead to reproducing churches spontaneously.

Many people fear that without the top-down model of leadership, there will be no clear authority. This is a false assumption based on bad experiences or lack of experience, or worse, a lack of understanding of how God designed his church to function. The strongest authority one can have is spiritual authority. If a person's life does not warrant them influence in the lives of others, then they won't be respected. But if they speak with wisdom and insight, and serve with a humble attitude, people will notice and will follow them, regardless of the person's title or position. Jesus led in this manner. He had authority in the lives of his disciples because of who he was, not a position or title he had. He operated outside the religious system of the day, but still was able to gather and lead his followers.

The strongest and most influential leaders do not need to rely on a title or position or being under someone else's 'covering'. It is the passion of these leaders, their character, their love for others, the sum total of who that person is, that gives them all the authority that is needed. Yes, it is important to be accountable to others. If you are in a top-down system of authority, either honour it or quietly and submissively withdraw. Do not stay and be a trouble-maker.

When I watched the film, *Braveheart*, for the first time, I was captivated by the example of a man without title or position but who led his nation. William Wallace (played by Mel Gibson) exercised unusual leadership. He stirred the hearts of his countrymen to rise up and fight for what they believed in. He did not have a formally recognized role of leadership, nor did he care for such things. Because of his passion, because of his willingness to sacrifice for what he believed, including a willingness to die for his beloved Scotland, he had the respect and affection of the people of Scotland. This is what spiritual authority is all about.

Neil Cole summarizes my favourite scene from *Braveheart* much better than I can:

> Wallace is speaking with Robert the Bruce, who is the true heir to the throne of Scotland. With passion, Wallace looked into his eyes and said, 'If you will only lead them, they will follow.' Then, with a glimmer of hope, he added extra punch by saying, 'And so would I.' For a revealing moment, the prince of Scotland was envious of the authority of a no-name son of a peasant who displayed true authority. He was visibly touched by the notion that this peasant warrior would follow him . . . One man had all the position and title, but the other had the authority. Leadership that rests on title is weak. Leadership that rests in a cause and inspires others to follow is not weak.

Leadership in simple church is like steering a ship

One person cannot single-handedly sail a ship much less guide a fleet of ships! If our dream is a movement of simple churches, it will take facilitative leaders within the churches, and a fluid team moving from community to community, to give it direction and input. Different communities will have members with a variety of gifts and strengths. As these men and women move among the churches, they are connected organically rather than by policies or rules. It takes a crew of people to navigate, set the sails, clean the decks and cook the food for such a movement. In fact, it will take many crews for many ships. That means team effort. It means creating a culture that encourages people to take initiative while learning to work with others to sail in the same direction. The role of each person in a team is vital for a ship to reach its destination. The responsibility of the helmsman is to point everyone in the same direction by involving the entire crew in the task at hand. Though each person on the crew has equal value, not every one has the same responsibility. It is the captain/helmsman who steers the ship, who brings the crew together and who inspires each person on board to fulfil his or her duties. Others can do the same thing from their place of serving on the ship.

God has provided the gift of leadership to the church. This gift is mentioned in 1 Corinthians 12:28 (where it is sometimes translated 'administration'), and comes from the Greek word *kubernesis*, which literally means to steer or pilot a sea-going vessel. While it is having a servant heart that qualifies a person for leadership, it is from words like *kubernesis* that we learn more about the responsibilities of those who step forward to lead. The same spiritual gift is referred to in Romans 12:8. In the Romans passage, Paul uses the word *proistimi*, which is often translated *to govern* or *to give oversight*. We call this the gift of leadership. The exercise of this gift should not be to the exclusion of others leading as well, from their area of strength.

Three responsibilities of those who lead in a simple-church community

Those that are given spiritual leadership are called to lead. In our concern about how a person leads, we need to be clear that the purpose of leadership is leading. It is going in front. It is making decisions and persuading others to be part of the decision. You can tell a leader because they have a following.

The exercise of spiritual authority differs according to the culture, gifts and personality of a person. While our culture will influence how we lead, it is our spiritual gifts that motivate what we do when we lead. The spiritual authority of a teacher flows from right use of the Scriptures to persuade and convince, whereas the prophet warns about sin in people's lives and asks penetrating questions. Apostolic authority is derived from the faith and vision the person has for new pioneering efforts. When Paul appeals to his authority as an apostle in correcting the believers in Corinth and Galatia, he is not thinking in terms of institutional or positional authority, but of his relationship to the believers as a spiritual father to them. He was not thinking in terms of hierarchy, but relationship and responsibility.

With these caveats and conditions in mind, it might be helpful to review the three primary responsibilities of those who lead in a local *ecclesia*. They are:

To guard

- Against 'wolves' from within – Acts 20:28–30
- Against false doctrine – 2 Timothy 4:1–5
- Against deceivers – 2 John 7–11
- Against those who cause divisions – Romans 16:17–18; Titus 3:10
- Against influences of sexual promiscuity – 1 Corinthians 5:9–13

To govern

- By caring for people – 'I have a special concern for you church leaders. I know what it's like to be a leader, in on Christ's sufferings as well as the coming glory. Here's my concern: that you care for God's flock with all the diligence of a shepherd. Not because you have to, but because you want to please God. Not calculating what you can get out of it, but acting spontaneously. Not bossily telling others what to do, but tenderly showing them the way.' 1 Peter 5:1–5, *The Message*
- By teaching God's word – 'Elders who do their work well should be paid well, especially those who work hard at both preaching and teaching.' 1 Timothy 5:17
- By correcting people in error – 'And the Lord's servant must not be quarrelsome but kindly to everyone, an apt teacher, patient, correcting opponents with gentleness. God may perhaps grant that they will repent and come to know the truth.' 2 Timothy 2:24–25

- By appointing other elders – Paul modelled and taught that elders appoint elders: 'I left you behind in Crete for this reason, so that you should put in order what remained to be done, and should appoint elders in every town, as I directed you.' Titus 1:5
- By making decisions – 'Command and teach these things . . . James spoke up: "Brothers, listen to me, it is my judgment ... then the apostles and elders, with the whole church, decided...' 1 Timothy 4:11; Acts 15:13–22

To guide

- By teaching the word – 'I solemnly urge you: proclaim the message; be persistent whether the time is favorable or unfavorable; convince, rebuke, and encourage, with the utmost patience in teaching . . . Now an overseer must be above reproach . . . able to teach...' 2 Timothy 4:1–2; 1 Timothy 3:2
- By discipling and equipping others to lead – 'And what you have heard from me through many witnesses entrust to faithful people who will be able to teach others as well . . . the gifts he gave were that some would be apostles, some prophets, some evangelists, some pastors and teachers, to equip the saints for the work of ministry...' 2 Timothy 2:2; Ephesians 4:11–12
- By imparting passion for God's glory to others – 'It has always been my ambition to preach the gospel where Christ is not known ... I urge you, brothers ... to join me in my struggle ... so that all nations might believe and obey him – to the only wise God be glory forever through Jesus Christ! Amen.' Romans 15:20, 30; 16:26–27

Leadership styles need to change in simple church

By understanding and being able to adapt one's leadership style, the dexterity of a leader increases. Such a person recognizes that different circumstances and different cultures call for different approaches to how we lead. We should always be servants in our attitude and character, but that does not mean we should always lead in the same manner. Jesus' style of leadership when he entered the Temple in outrage at the injustices done by the Temple priests and money changers was directive. He told people what to do, to say the least:

> Jesus went straight to the Temple and threw out everyone who had set up shop, buying and selling. He kicked over the tables of loan sharks and the stalls of dove merchants. . .[6]

But when the disciples were disputing about their place of honour in his kingdom, Jesus was kind to them, coaching them in the right attitude and understanding. He welcomed little children to sit on his lap as he illustrated what it meant to be great in his kingdom.[7]

Many leaders make the mistake of thinking leadership is equal to being able to give directives. That is true if it is about task authority in the workplace, or has to do with dealing with an emergency – such as an airline pilot when there is a crisis – but it does not work that way with spiritual authority.

Simple church by its size and nature needs a coaching and supporting leadership style, not a directing or delegating manner of leading. The box below illustrates the four basic leadership styles:

support	coach
delegate	direct

---

[6] Matthew 21:12, *The Message*
[7] Luke 9:46–48

People have a natural style, according to their personality and culture and upbringing. To not be aware of one's natural leadership style will most likely cause a leader to be a prisoner of their own personality. Self-awareness allows a mature person to adjust how they lead, so they can serve people more effectively. My natural style is directive. Though I love to inspire people, I naturally lean towards accomplishing tasks and getting things done. I have both ingredients in me. It is how I was wired in my personality and make-up. While giving orders would enable me to be a good boss on a chain gang, it does not work well in inspiring people to be part of organic church. I have had to learn to adopt a coaching and supportive style of leading to be the servant leader I want to be. That has meant dying to my self, more times than I like to think about. But it is the right thing to do. It has made me more effective, and more sensitive to others. It has allowed me to connect to people's hearts, and to coach and support those I lead. That doesn't take away the responsibility from others to be appropriately submissive, but it does make it easier for them!

Submission to spiritual, task and teaching authority

The dominant value in our culture today is freedom, usually accompanied by a big dose of cynicism and mistrust towards authority figures. Freedom is certainly the greatest value among postmoderns. It is not surprising, therefore, when young adults come to Christ that they struggle with being 'under authority', particularly where there is no relationship with the one leading. Different generations in the church think differently about spiritual authority. While baby boomers in America have a history of challenging authority, succeeding generations have questioned the need for any authority.

It is important to teach new believers the true nature of spiritual authority, i.e. servanthood, and the value of allowing themselves to be served by godly leaders. A father in the Lord, Tom

Marshall, once said, 'We live in freedom only within the constraints of divine order in all of our relationships.' What is the divine order Tom wrote about, and how does it work?

> **We live in freedom only within the constraints of divine order in all of our relationships.**

I have grave misgivings regarding the teaching of being 'under covering' and serious concerns about the way some teach about being in 'submission to authority'. We need to think very carefully about what the Bible teaches in regard to these subjects. It seems the easiest way to deal with the issue of spiritual authority is to avoid it, or to shy away from a church that expects submission and accountability, or on the other extreme to teach a hierarchical version of top-down, command-and-control authority. But the answer is not found in either extreme.

The Bible makes it clear that we are to be committed to a local community of Jesus-followers.[8] Being part of a simple-church community includes submission to true spiritual authority, which means we are humble enough to allow ourselves to be served by others with spiritual gifts we don't have. Some have erroneously taught that to be part of a simple church or house church, is to be free from all spiritual authority. In fact, submission to a person or a group of people who follow Jesus is a sign of spiritual maturity. That includes submitting to those who lead. However, there is a difference between submission and blind obedience. Obedience for the sake of obedience is not good. We can obey evil as well as good; we can obey man when we ought to obey God. Nor is obedience that produces conformity biblical obedience. Obedience to spiritual leaders in order to gain acceptance feeds an unhealthy need for approval.

---

[8] Hebrews 12:25; Ephesians 4:16; James 2:2; Acts 2:40–47; 11:26; 20:20;

Three kinds of authority

It was Tom Marshall who taught the difference between three varying kinds of authority and the obedience that is appropriate to each one:[9]

1. Task authority
2. Teaching authority
3. Spiritual authority

Submission to authority is to be exercised differently in each of these categories. Many of the problems regarding submission to leaders arises from not understanding these differences, or confusing their use and application. Let's take a look at each one of them.

Task authority

This is the simplest and easiest to understand. This kind of authority has to do with a job that is to be done. A person put in charge of a task or projects gives assignments and direction; under him or her is a group of people whose responsibility is to comply with the leader's instructions as promptly and efficiently as they can. It may or may not be appropriate to be 'creative' in fulfilling those responsibilities, or to take time to discuss the pros and cons of how to do the tasks assigned to us. In a work situation, sometimes we just need to be told what to do and do it. Kindly, of course!

Task authority is a legitimate and effective form of leadership. It welds a group of individuals into a single operating unit, and allows work to be done efficiently. The New Testament uses the Greek word *peitharcheo* (to obey a chief or ruler) to describe the obedience that is appropriate in response to those in charge in

---

[9] Tom Marshall, *Understanding Leadership*, Regal 1998.

work situations.[10] This word is also used to describe the kind of obedience we are to give to government leaders.[11]

Teaching authority

When we consider submission to teaching authority, the purpose is much more than simply accomplishing a task. Teaching authority is not about something to be done, but truth to be learned. What is of greatest importance is that the one learning has the opportunity to internalize what is being taught and make it part of themselves. In these situations, unlike task authority, questions and answers, reasons, explanations and dealing with objections and misunderstandings are all part of the learning process. The Bible uses the Greek word *peitho* (to be persuaded) to describe the kind of response God is looking for to someone teaching the Bible. God wants obedience to truth *with understanding*. God wants us to respond from the heart. When the writer to the Hebrews says, 'obey your leaders',[12] *peitho* is the word he uses. This passage is about teaching authority, not task or spiritual authority. Unfortunately, this passage is often quoted to support dominating leaders.

Teaching authority is based on the ability to persuade. We can convince others by appealing to God's word and to our story, with the aim that those who are taught have revelation for themselves. Paul said, 'Therefore, knowing the fear of the Lord, we try to *persuade* others...'.[13] Remember, 90 per cent of what people remember and apply to their own lives comes through self-discovery. The teacher may teach, but there has to come a moment when the light goes on in a person's mind by the work of the Holy Spirit. Those 'aha' moments are what effective teachers live for.

[10] Titus 3:1

[11] Romans 13:1

[12] Hebrews 13:17

[13] 2 Corinthians 5:11

Teaching authority is based on the ability to persuade ... the aim is that those who are taught must have revelation for themselves.

Teaching authority in the church is often confused with task and spiritual authority. The pastor or leader who balks at being asked legitimate questions needs to understand the difference between the different types of authority. Applying task authority to teaching authority will not produce true learning. It actually does real harm by hindering true learning, and tempts people to say what is expected of them to stay in good standing with their leaders.

Spiritual authority

The aim of spiritual authority is different from teaching and task authority. The purpose of spiritual authority is not passive compliance, but for people to be motivated from the heart by Jesus' commands. Those with spiritual authority have responsibilities to guard, govern and guide those they are given authority to lead. Their task is made easier if those they lead submit to their leadership. If their leadership is exercised in a mature manner, they will seek to influence those they lead to hear God for themselves and obey him from the heart. Spiritual growth happens through self-discovery, not imposed obedience. The purpose of spiritual authority is to inspire people to obey the commands of Jesus and to equip them for service, not command or control people's lives.

The purpose of spiritual authority is to inspire people to obey the commands of Jesus and to equip them for service, not command or control people's lives.

The essence of Christian maturity is a response from the heart to the will of God and to the direction given by spiritual leaders. If a person alters their behaviour for any other reason than a loving response to God, e.g. to please their leaders, it is not obedience that pleases God nor does it make for healthy community.

The word for spiritual authority is *hupakouo*, 'to listen under'. This does not mean to listen under others, but to listen from under the surface in one's heart, to hear God from deep within. Hearing and obeying God comes from under the surface, from deep within the heart. A spiritual leader may be a channel of God's Spirit motivating a person, but that person still needs to internalize what God is saying *to them*. Telling a person what they must do, and why they should not do something else, may get a leader the immediate results he or she wants, but it doesn't produce spiritual maturity in others.

The exercise of spiritual authority in relation to this kind of obedience should be aimed at helping a person discover the will of God by hearing God themselves. If people know how to hear God themselves, then spontaneously reproducing movements of simple churches is much more likely to happen. Top-down spiritual authority stifles a movement, making the leaders the bottleneck through which all decisions must pass. But when people hear God for themselves, they can get on with the work God has called all of us to do.

Perhaps it is helpful to summarize the nature of spiritual authority this way:

○ Derived authority: the authority that has to do with earning the right to lead others. Derived authority is the consequence of godly character, wisdom, servanthood, humility, and recognition by others of a person's gifting and calling.
○ Delegated authority: the authority given to a person by someone else. A person with delegated authority must also earn the right to lead people spiritually.

○ Distributed authority: the authority given by Jesus to all those who know, love and obey him. It is distributed to everyone in the church but is only effective if it is exercised in humble obedience to the commands of Jesus. All those who are Christ-like share in the spiritual authority that Jesus gives to all his children.

There are conditions and qualifications in order for spiritual authority to be exercised properly. For example, the Bible is careful to distinguish between spiritual authority in the church and the authority of government leaders. The authority that Paul speaks about in Romans 13 is the *right* and *power* to enforce obedience by government officials. But the authority Peter speaks about in 1 Peter 5 is the *responsibility* spiritual leaders have to serve God's people with love and integrity, not the power to command or control those they lead.

Below are a list of scriptures that clarify the scope of authority spiritual leaders have been given by God, with clear conditions and restrictions:

1 Peter 5:1–5 Now as an elder myself and a witness of the sufferings of Christ, as well as one who shares in the glory to be revealed, I exhort the elders among you to tend the flock of God that is in your charge, exercising oversight, not under compulsion but willingly, as God would have you do it—not for sordid gain but eagerly. Do not lord it over those in your charge, but be examples to the flock. And when the chief shepherd appears, you will win the crown of glory that never fades away. In the same way, you who are younger must accept the authority of the elders. And all of you must clothe yourselves with humility in your dealings with one another, for God opposes the proud, but gives grace to the humble.

1 Timothy 5:17 Let the elders who rule well be considered worthy of double honour, especially those who labour in preaching and teaching.

Titus 1:5 I left you behind in Crete for this reason, so that you should put in order what remained to be done, that you should appoint elders in every town, as I directed you.

Acts 20:28–31 Keep watch over yourselves and over all the flock, of which the Holy Spirit has made you overseers, to shepherd the church of God that he obtained with the blood of his own Son. I know that after I have gone, savage wolves will come in among you, not sparing the flock. Some even from your own group will come distorting the truth in order to entice the disciples to follow them. Therefore be alert, remembering that for three years I did not cease night or day to warn everyone with tears.

1 Thessalonians 5:12–13 And now, friends, we ask you to honour those leaders who work so hard for you, who have been given the responsibility of urging and guiding you in your obedience. Overwhelm them with appreciation and love!

Hebrews 13:17 Obey your leaders and submit to them . . . Let them do this with joy and not with sighing – for that would be harmful to you.

2 Timothy 4:1–2 In the presence of God and of Christ Jesus, who is to judge the living and the dead, and in view of his appearing and his kingdom, I solemnly urge you: proclaim the message; be persistent whether the time is favorable or unfavourable; convince, rebuke, and encourage, with the utmost patience in teaching.

2 Timothy 2:24–25 And the Lord's servant must not be quarrelsome but kindly to everyone, an apt teacher, patient, correcting opponents with gentleness. God may perhaps grant that they will repent and come to know the truth.

The real question concerning spiritual authority is not whether it exists, but how is it to be exercised and our response to it. Jesus made it abundantly clear that what he meant by authority was different from what the spiritual leaders of the day thought was their authority. Jesus defined authority as influencing people by serving them. If we serve we have influence, and if we influence people, we have spiritual authority in their lives.[14] In this way,

---

[14] Luke 22:26–27

authority is defined as the privilege of influencing others by exercising one's spiritual gifts in a Christ-like manner.

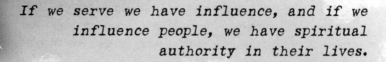

If we serve we have influence, and if we influence people, we have spiritual authority in their lives.

But how do we know if we are exercising spiritual authority the way Jesus did? The following 'authority' tests may help:

○ does it liberate or does it enslave?
○ does it lead to conformity or does it bring creativity?
○ does it bring dependence on man or God?
○ does it produce servility or servanthood?
○ does it depend on law or grace?
○ does it destroy or does it build a person's confidence?
○ does it equip people to function in faith or does it produce fear?
○ does it produce accountability or anarchy?
○ does it equip people for ministry or does it make them spectators to the ministries of others?

Team leadership

I believe in team leadership. Dick Iverson, spiritual father to a movement of over 1,000 churches, has taught on team leadership for many years. Dick believes in appointing elders who lead together under the leadership of a recognized team leader. Dick says that elders in the New Testament served as peers, and as peers, they cared for the flock. Dick believes there was not just one pastor, as is common today.[15] I agree.

Each person needs opportunity and encouragement to serve side by side with their gifts and passions. Just how does diversity

---

[15] Dick Iverson, *Team Ministry*, City Bible Publishing 1989, p 40.

on a team glorify God? There is a unique honour God receives from a team of people who subordinate their individual personalities and perspectives to work together. It requires each team member to work through his or her differences and fears. The glory God receives from a team learning to work in such a way is much greater than that which comes from one-person leadership models. Each team member has to accept the invitation to go to the cross with each new challenge the team faces. Dying to one's rights, preferences, mistrust, and old ways of relating is the price to pay for team unity.

Through years of working on teams, I have concluded that it takes five to seven years to achieve a deep level of trust and unity on a team. Team members as individuals and as a whole must learn to speak truth to other members of the team. Biblical principles of speech must be followed, forgiveness given, and personal trust developed. Such trust is not based on performance or perfection, but on growing together in truth and grace. New Testament leadership is team-oriented.

Harnessing the gifts and callings of a group of strong-willed, gifted and opinionated leaders takes a major work of grace on the part of each member of the team. It can be done but not without the leader getting involved in each of the team member's lives, spouses included. It takes years of sacrifice, humility and continuing growth on the part of each member of the team for it to work.

I am zealous about team ministry because working together in unity is just as important to God as what we do for him. How we treat each other, the depth and honesty of our relationships, is a reflection of our ultimate team leader, the Lord Jesus. If we are obedient followers of Christ, then we do ministry the way he modelled for us to do it.

I believe in team ministry because it gets at the very heart of what it means to be and do simple church. We are the family of God, and as such we are designed and called by God to function in family units. One-man leadership models do not fulfil what we are taught in the Scriptures nor do they glorify God as much as leading in teams. Team leadership is a form of simple church; it is a group of men and women sharing their lives with each other in order to fulfil the great commission and the great commandment.

> *I believe in team ministry because I believe the journey is as important as the end goal.*

I believe in team ministry because it helps us grow spiritually. It confronts our flesh patterns and exposes our brokenness. Working with a team of strong-willed leaders pushes all our 'buttons'. When we work side by side, making decisions, initiating projects, supervising people, gathering small groups, discipling and evangelizing together, acting and reacting to each other, we get to know one another at a deep level. We can't hide our stuff in the close spiritual quarters of team life. We have to open up our hearts to each other if we are to lead as a cohesive unit. Building such a team takes time and transparency. It means working through conflicts privately and openly as a team. We have to be willing to open our hearts to each other, learn to trust, be open to adjustment, and get used to humbling ourselves a lot. If you are willing to not get your way on occasion, to give in to others, you will enjoy team ministry.

I believe in team ministry because I believe the journey is as important as the end goal. If all Father wants from us is results, he would have created robots. But he wants a spiritual family, not a well-oiled machine. He wants to build redeemed people into a community of connected hearts and lives, not just well-run programmes that reduce church life to watching others do their thing.

Team ministry is contrary to Western, goal-oriented, individualistic ways of doing things. We have come to believe in the West that inefficiency is a sin against the Holy Ghost. If we run churches like corporations, and church programmes like assembly lines, we can get results, but at what price?

We have come to believe in the West that inefficiency is a sin against the Holy Ghost.

Modern evangelicals have mastered the techniques of building big churches, but are they New Testament churches they are building? They know how to manage church growth, but if someone took away the buildings and the programmes, what would be left? Technique-oriented Christianity takes the soul out of church. And who needs a soulless Christianity in a postmodern world?

I believe in team ministry because it gets us to the soul of what church is all about. It is a way of building community by modelling church as family. It imparts to a church or movement the spirit and values of what it means to be *ecclesia*. God designed the church to function as a body, as a family, and naturally that requires genuine relationships. The organs of our body cannot function alone and fulfil their purpose. Nor can prophets or apostles or teachers function that way either. We are made to work together, 'individually members of one another.'[16]

I believe in team ministry because it calls us to deep levels of trust. Trust is vital for a healthy team. Absence of trust stems from an unwillingness to be vulnerable with one another, by taking time to work through differences and conflicts in an open and humble fashion. Team members who are not open with one another about their fears, their hurts and their sinful tendencies make it impossible to build a foundation of trust. Patrick Lencioni, in his brilliant book, *The Five Dysfunctions of a Team*, defines trust as 'believing the other members of the team have my well being

---

[16] Romans 12:4–5

in mind'.[17] Trust means I want people to help me by speaking into my area of ministry, my personal performance, and into the deep places of my heart. It means inviting and welcoming input from others on the team. Trust means I submit the important decisions I make to my co-workers in an open and direct manner.

Failure to build trust in a team is damaging because it hinders healthy debate, resulting in little or no heart-felt commitment to decisions, avoidance of mutual accountability, and getting side-tracked from our mission. Without trust a team cannot be a team, certainly not a team that reflects the love that exists between the Father, Son and Holy Spirit. A team without trust and mutual submission cannot experience the oneness of heart and mind that Paul calls the 'mind of Christ'.[18]

I believe in team ministry because it facilitates mutual account-ability. I don't believe in top-down accountability, where the leader is responsible for getting everyone to toe the line. Mutual accountability is the natural result of uncensored debate, waiting on God together, healthy patterns of truth talking, meeting with two or three others to share burdens and confess sins, and own-ing the decisions that are made by the team.

Two caveats about team ministry: team is not a panacea for all the challenges facing a simple-church community. In other words, it is not an end in itself. Secondly, team ministry is almost impos-sible where the team leader is not a father to those on the team. More to the point, when a team leader inherits team members, there is little likelihood the team will be able to function without a profound work of God in the team members' hearts.

Leaders need friends too

God said it is not good for a man to be alone.[19] In fact, God said this before Adam and Eve fell into sin. He does not want us to be

---

[17] Patrick Lencioni, *The Five Dysfunctions of a Team*, Jossey-Bass (Wiley) 2002, p 30.
[18] Philippians 2:1–3   [19] Genesis 2:18

alone in marriage or ministry. Friendship with loyal team members and a few close friends in the church family keeps us alive. It protects us from yielding to temptation when everything in us wants to give up.

Jesus did not trust himself to the crowds, or the followers who came out of the crowds. He knew the difference between a follower and a friend. And we must as well.

A warning: crowds of people who want to speak into your life don't equal quality friendships. Having numerous people in your life can actually prevent the development of significant friendships. Jesus designed team ministry to deal with this quandary. He modelled the solution for us. He preached to the crowds, but he built his friendships with a few close associates. He invested most of his time and energy in the lives of those he worked most closely with, and they became his friends.[20] Jesus did not trust himself to the crowds, or the followers who came out of the crowds.[21] He knew the difference between a follower and a friend. And we must, as well.

We can and should build friendships with those we disciple. Every effective leader invests in the lives of a few people at a time. In-depth personal discipleship takes the sting out of the 'lonely leader' syndrome and creates a culture of friendship and community in our church. As I write these words, I am thinking about a few friends I am investing in on a regular basis. I love hanging out with Nelis, Danny, Robert and Renee, Cobus and Marlize, Gawie and others in our movement. I trust them, and because I trust

---

[20] John 15:15

[21] John 2:24 says, 'But Jesus did not commit himself to them, because he knew all men. . .'

them, they are my friends. Genuine personal discipleship involves friendship. You can't invest yourself in someone's life without becoming friends. Paul said, 'We loved you so much that we gave you not only God's Good News but our own lives, too.'[22]

This gets a little complicated for me personally because I wear multiple 'hats'. I am a spiritual leader, at times a project manager, and a friend. Because I am someone's project supervisor doesn't mean I have to be their best friend. But quality friendships must be part of a team if it's to be effective. There are times when I have to say no to a co-worker. When that happens I sometimes must take off my friend hat, and speak firmly about what I believe is right for everyone involved. That kind of talk is a test for friends and co-workers, but talking truth with each other is absolutely essential if we are to grow together as real friends and healthy co-workers.

Is this too difficult to do? Not for Jesus, and not for us either if we are willing to grow in the skill and honesty it requires. That doesn't mean we have to be best friends with everyone we work with, but we should work towards good friendships with all those we work closely with. It's not possible if there is a lack of trust, but where there is humility and transparency, there will be growing friendships.

Apostolic teams and their role

The primary difference between a leader's role in a simple-church community and an apostolic team, is vision and function. Elders in a simple church serve to equip and disciple the members of the church, or network of churches, they serve. Apostolic teams focus on pioneering amongst those who have not yet heard the good news, moving throughout a network of churches. Apostolic teams give oversight to pioneering movements. They cultivate

---

[22] 1 Thessalonians 2:8, NLT

and uphold a set of core values that empower such a movement. Local church elders care for the flock under their charge; an apostolic team does the same thing but also cultivates a church-planting culture of faith and vision for those who have never heard the good news.

> *Apostolic teams give oversight to pioneering movements. They cultivate and uphold a set of core values that empower such a movement.*

Apostolic teams are focused. They are not satisfied with just overseeing the affairs of a local church. They burn with a desire to plant churches and reach those outside the influence of the gospel, especially those who have never heard of God's love in Christ. Apostolic teams are not apostolic because the team members are prophets or apostles. They are apostolic because they have a vision to plant churches where the gospel has not yet been proclaimed. You can be an apostle by gifting and fail to fulfil the purpose of your gift. Apostles are pioneers by calling, but they start new churches to fulfil their calling.

I have a very simple way of defining apostolic teams: they do what apostles did in the book of Acts. They preach the gospel, make disciples for Christ, plant churches and appoint and coach elders of local churches. They believe God for the impossible and pull down Satan's strongholds. They suffer and sacrifice for what they believe in. In short, they win, gather, and multiply disciples and churches for Jesus – especially where people are unchurched and unreached.

Apostolic teams typically are linked to a leader with an apostolic gifting, although sometimes it is the combination of gifts on a team that makes it apostolic. The key to being an apostolic team is that you do the stuff apostles did! Paul said, '. . . I make it my ambition to preach the gospel, not where Christ has already been named. . .'[23] If your team has that ambition, you can function as an apostolic team.

You can talk about being apostolic until you're blue in the face, but if you don't plant and reproduce churches you're not apostolic. If you worship and fast together to hear God's plans and strategies for the lost, and then lay hands on those God appoints to be sent out,[24] you have the beginnings of an apostolic team.[25]

> *You can talk about being apostolic until you're blue in the face, but if you don't plant and reproduce churches you're not apostolic.*

Death benefits: The price of leading a dry-bones army

Death benefits. I heard that term once when someone was trying to sell me insurance. I didn't buy the insurance, but I do buy the concept. I believe in death benefits. There are huge benefits to dying to self. One of the best ways to reap those benefits is to serve others. Leading in the simple-church model I have presented in this book is not complicated.

> *Do you want to stand out? Then step down.*

Leading in the 'dry-bones' army of simple church is not complicated – if we are not doing it for recognition. That's the death benefit. We get to die to ourselves. Leading is not about us finding our ministry. It's about bringing life and hope to others.

---

[23] Romans 15:20

[24] A study of the missionary journeys of Paul makes it abundantly clear that the one thing he consistently accomplished was the preaching of the gospel and the establishing of new churches.

[25] Acts 13:1–3

God calls people to lead for his sake, and the sake of others, not ours. Practically speaking, that means equipping and releasing those we serve into a life of 'skilled servant work'. Paul understood this concept of leading as a doorway to death benefits. He called it a 'sentence of death'. He described it in this way:

> We felt like we'd been sent to death row, that it was all over for us. As it turned out, it was the best thing that could have happened. Instead of trusting in our own strength or wits to get out of it, we were forced to trust God totally – not a bad idea since he's the God who raises the dead![26]

We are called to die. Not just once to sin, but as a way of life. By dying to 'our' rights, we find life. That means dying to our opinions, dying to the right to be understood, the right to be represented, the right to be loved, the right to be treated justly, and all our other rights. Very few leaders understand this truth. They strive to find their role, their ministry, how they fit on the team, etc. It is sad to watch men and women strive to keep what they have to give up anyway if they are to be part of God's mission. Jim Elliot wrote in his journal, 'He is no fool who gives up what he cannot keep to gain what he cannot lose.'

It would be easy at this point to go on without considering the implications of this truth. But would you mind pausing for a moment and reflecting with me on God's invitation to die? It is an invitation. We are not forced to live like this. We don't have to serve others. We can hide in the dry-bones army and not volunteer. We can be a superstar-type leader and avoid dying to self. We can go to heaven without getting to this place in our walk with God. Serving is key to the new way of doing church. The old way is about rights, about position, about 'running the church'. But to be part of the dry-bones army we learn to live for his glory, not ours. That means serving from underneath, not on top.

---

[26] 2 Corinthians 1:9, *The Message*

Paul accepted being sent to 'death row' because he learned that it put him in a place where he had to trust God. As you take the time to pray about the 'death benefits' in this new way of doing church, consider the following:

○ Death benefits mean giving up control over my time. Am I willing to make a commitment to set aside time each day to read God's word and pray? Not just driving time, or walking-around-the-house prayer time, but time I give up doing something else to be alone with Jesus?

○ Death benefits mean purity. Am I willing to make a pledge to God and others to live a life of sexual and moral purity, including the kinds of music I listen to and the films I watch? Will I stay away from all forms of pornography, including on the Internet?

○ Death benefits mean dying to my rights. Am I willing to give up all personal rights?

○ Death benefits mean accountability to others. Am I willing to invite others to speak into the important decisions of my life before I make them? That includes decisions that will affect my church community and co-workers. Am I willing to be known in areas of personal holiness?

○ Death benefits include being committed and loyal to a small community of people that invest in one another's lives through personal discipleship and accountability – are you willing to accept this death benefit in the kingdom of God?

○ Death benefits include telling people about Jesus without regard to personal reputation or ambition. Am I willing to share Jesus with my neighbours, family members and others in my sphere of influence, as a way of life?

○ Death benefits mean embracing sacrifice and suffering. Am I willing to live sacrificially, even suffer for him so others can hear about Jesus? Am I willing to give up my country, my comfort, what is familiar, so others can know Jesus?

Finding my ministry?

I spent quite a few years as a young man preoccupied with finding my ministry. I was asking the wrong questions most of the time, searching for the wrong thing, focusing on the wrong person.

Asking the wrong questions can be a huge distraction to finding one's ministry. If we are to change the way we do church, if we are to be leaders in the simple army of God, it starts by laying down our lives, not striving to find them. But that is getting ahead of the story.

4

The Next Bono – or is it Billy Graham?

When I was younger I desperately wanted to know what I was going to do with my life. When I reflect on that stage of my life, I have to admit I was pretty occupied with myself. I swung back and forth between different great things I could picture myself doing for God. One day I wanted to be the next Billy Graham, preaching to stadiums full of lost sinners eager to hear me proclaim the good news. I'm sure if Bono and U2 were around then, I would have dreamed about leading the greatest rock band of all time. But in actuality the only thing Bono and I have in common is Irish ancestry.

At other moments of messianic delusion, I decided my real destiny was to become the next John Stott, one of the great Bible teachers of my day. When I was in university, I decided I was going to be a martyr in the Amazon jungles, just like Jim Elliot. I'm not sure if you can actually choose to be a martyr, but that was what I thought about and prayed for.[1]

During my Billy Graham phase, I listened to all the Billy sermons I could get hold of. I watched him on TV. I saw how people

---

[1] I was deeply impacted by the life of Jim Elliot. Jim's story is told by his widow, Elisabeth Elliot, in *The Shadow of the Almighty*, reissue edn., HarperSanFrancisco, 1989.

responded when he invited them to get out of their seats and come forward. George Beverly Shea sang 'Just As I Am' and people streamed down by the thousands to accept Jesus. I figured if Billy could do it, so could I. We serve the same God, right? I thought it might help to hold my Bible like Billy did when he preached. I held it out in front of me, open, and I pointed my finger like Billy, and said, 'The Bible says. . .'. I preached and walked back and forth on the platform just like he did it. And then I made the altar call. I stood back and bowed my head, folded my arms with one hand on my chin, praying quietly. I tried to be as humble and expectant as I could. And guess what happened? Nothing. No one came. Actually, sometimes one or two came, but they didn't stream forward by the thousands like they do when Billy preaches. It's a little embarrassing to discover you're not the next Billy Graham.

Like a lot of young adults my age, I had spiritual ambition. But I lacked perspective, and not a little humility. I knew God had called me to leadership, but I had failed to understand what form that would take, or the price to find it. I definitely was not interested in the 'death benefits' of the kingdom of God in those days. I have been a natural leader since I was a child. I organized other kids on the playground when we chose teams and played sports. I appointed myself to be parental supervisor of my sister and brother, to their chagrin. I was captain of the basketball team in high school. I ran for student body president in university and won. I led a half-way house in Afghanistan by the time I was 26.

> *I knew God had called me to leadership, but I had failed to understand what form that would take.*

All my life my people have looked to me when it came time to decide what we were going to do. I was a leader but I was woefully ignorant of God's ways in leadership. I didn't understand how God called and then developed leaders. I didn't know the ways of God in testing a leader. At times I was ahead of my character development in the levels of responsibility I was given. I lacked the wisdom to know that.

Looking for a spiritual father

During that time I had a longing for a spiritual father or mother to understand me, give me some guidance and perspective, and walk me through the process of figuring out my 'anointing' from God. I really didn't know what the anointing was, but I had heard it preached from the pulpit and assumed it had to do with God's calling on my life to leadership.

Fortunately, God put some amazing people in my life to disciple and instruct me. During one period of questioning when we lived in Afghanistan, God sent a woman of God I respected at just the right time. She had been a mentor and spiritual mother to me from a distance, but I needed someone up close to ask questions and talk through the questions I was asking. I shared with her my longing to discover God's ministry direction for my life. Would I be an evangelist like Billy Graham? A missionary like Jim Elliot? A Bible teacher like John Stott? A pastor, maybe? She wisely listened to my longings and frustrations, asked lots of questions about my dreams and passions, and then explained the characteristics of the five leadership giftings described by Paul in Ephesians 4: pastor, teacher, evangelist, prophet, apostle. She didn't tell me what my gifts were, but pointed me in the right direction to discover answers for myself. Wisely, she was not telling me what she thought my lifelong ministry would be, but she did point me to the gifts that motivated one's ministry.

As I studied Paul's description of the five functions of equipping leadership in Ephesians 4, and as I read other passages in the Bible about leadership, I began to get some insight for myself. I recognized myself in some of the spiritual gifts Paul wrote about.

In fact, my heart really came alive when I read about Paul's pioneering exploits in the book of Acts. I identified with Paul travelling from place to place, preaching and gathering new believers. His courage to lead, to challenge the status quo, and pioneer new beachheads for the kingdom of God inspired me to lead courageously.

For a long time I had been critical about the church and its problems. But being thrust by God into a pioneering work among dropped-out young people got me out of the complaining mode and into the action mode. I had to stop whining and lead. I couldn't blame others for what was not happening: I was the leader! So I prayed a lot and worked hard and that kept me focused on believing God for breakthroughs in the lives of those we were reaching out to. I was experiencing God's blessing on my life. Small victories in our ministry gave me courage to take on bigger challenges. Like David who fought a lion and bear before he faced Goliath, God was giving me my own bears and lions to face and conquer. Most of the battles we fought were for people to be set free from sin and spiritual bondage. We fasted, prayed, and persisted in faith for drug addicts and others who were wounded and lost, separated by many miles from their family and their country. Like Ezekiel, we were reaching out to young men and women who in effect said, 'Our bones are dry, our hope is lost. . .'[2]

Talk about an army of dry bones; the young people we were taking into our home were really hurting. Many of them came from broken homes. Most of them started sleeping around when they were barely teenagers. They had experimented with drugs and alcohol at an early age. There was a cloud of spiritual death, lifelessness actually, hanging over their lives. But slowly, one by one, they came to Jesus. And he breathed life into them. They loved community. They listened as we taught about the church in

---

[2] Ezekiel 37:11

the book of Acts, and they connected what happened in the early church with how we were living. They saw what we were doing as church. They responded to my leadership and that gave me confidence.

> *You might say God tricked us into loving the church by teaching us to love the people we were taking into our home. We discovered that, for them, we were the church.*

It was tough working with disillusioned young people, but we were having fun. People were coming to Jesus regularly. Their lives were being transformed, and we were discovering a new way of doing church. We discovered church was community – it was like having an extended family. You might say God tricked us into loving the church by teaching us to love the people we were taking into our home. We discovered that, for them, we were the church. And in the process of loving them, our gifts of leadership developed.

I discovered in those days that I loved pioneering and I loved community, but I had many questions I could not find answers to. I thrived on the challenge of doing something other people said was impossible. Where others saw impossibilities, I saw opportunities. I learned that I had the ability to inspire vision and faith in people for the vision God put in my heart. As I led our community, and as I responded to the questions my mentors asked me, and as I studied the word, I came to the conclusion that the gift that I most closely identified with was apostolic leadership. I was excited when I read about the apostles planting churches and pioneering new efforts to tell people about Jesus. But the idea also confused me. I had read somewhere that there were no modern-day apostles; that the gift of apostleship had ended with the first generation of Christians.

I share this part of my story because I believe there are many leaders who are equally confused about their ministry and how it fits in conventional church life. I came to a place where I realized that my gifts did not fit in conventional church, but it took a long time to be secure in that discovery. If you are confused, or lack confidence in who you are and how you are to do church, I hope my story will help you be all God has called you to be. Perhaps you are not the problem, but the way church and leadership in the church has been modelled to you is the problem.

In one very significant way I don't identify with the early apostles, at least not Paul. I more easily identify with Barnabas or Timothy. I was insecure about my gifting and calling much more than I was confident. I didn't have the confidence of Paul, though I yearned for the same results. My struggle to find my gifting would have been helped along had I found a good book on the subject of alternative church and missional leadership. Not about conventional church, but church as a movement and a radical community. In fact, I read everything I could get my hands on about the Moravians, the early Methodists, and the Anabaptists. I sensed that I was more a spiritual descendant of Zinzendorf and Menno Simons and Wesley than Calvin or Luther.

Ephesians 4 says that Jesus gave pastors and prophets and teachers and evangelists and apostles to equip others to do the work of ministry. Unfortunately, there is a certain aura or status associated with the term 'apostle' in church culture. No doubt it's because that's the term Jesus used for the original twelve disciples. They performed miracles, saw Jesus in his resurrected body, cast out demons and healed the sick. They had powerful anointings from God. I can understand why some who are called to apostolic ministry today may be tempted to borrow on the authority of the early apostles. Perhaps they feel if they call themselves an apostle it will help matters. My view is that people overuse the term 'apostle' to give themselves a boost, rather than being secure in being themselves. I've concluded that the more a person has to announce their ministry, the more insecure they are about it. It's not that it's improper to know your gifts and calling. It's overdoing the titles and introductions that's the problem. A Bible teacher who knows their calling and has the assurance and confidence of a man or woman who enjoys God's blessing in their life, doesn't have to put 'Bible Teacher' on their business card, or insist on being called 'Apostle Smith'.

I definitely didn't want 'Apostle McClung' on my business card! Besides, in those days I didn't have a business card. I just wanted to understand my place in the body. Part of what I was going through was motivated by insecurity, and part of it was a sincere desire to understand what I was going to do with my life. It was a pretty lonely struggle. There were no popular books written about the subject, and I didn't feel comfortable talking about it with others besides the few mentors I felt I could open up with.

It takes guts to change the way you do church

What does this have to do with changing the way we do church? We need people who will challenge the way things have always been done. Unless a few men or women step forward with the guts to change the way we do church, we won't know what might be. That means experimenting, being innovative, going on a journey with Jesus and a few friends into the unknown. It means experimenting and taking risks with how we do church.

It means that some of us are going to have to live somewhere between the old and the new. It probably will mean living with a few contradictions between the old way and the new way of doing church until you find your way forward. I lived with those tensions for many years while I searched for the new way to do church. I set out on a journey, determined to find a new way, a better way to reach people. I was convinced that there was a seamless connection in God's heart between the church and God's mission for the church, but I wasn't sure of what that looked like.

So I launched out, experiencing quite a bit of misunderstanding and rejection. We tried different approaches, and still are trying them. We asked ourselves, 'Are we a missions agency? An organization? What are we?' I have settled on 'movement', though some have ridiculed our use of that term. But no one can question our desire to be a movement. I have discovered that, because I have a dream in my heart of what the church is called to be, I am not the prisoner of those who don't share my dream. I dare to dream because God has deposited some courage in my heart. It is his grace to me, and I receive that grace to follow my dream.

While you search for the way forward, holding on to what is good from the past, looking for the new way in the future, what will help you arrive at the new way of doing church is a set of core values that guide you. You need to look to the future with 'apostolic eyes', as one young leader called it. Vision is often about where we are going in the future. The trouble with a vision that is not yet clear is that it is not yet clear! Meanwhile, what will give certainty is core values, inner passions that keep you motivated and connected to Jesus.

It was a set of core values that I aspired to that kept me motivated as I questioned the old and searched for the new. As I pondered the meaning of what an apostolic calling looked like, and how that would affect the way I understood and did church, one thing became clear to me. The early apostles had courage. They were known for their boldness.[3] Though they were beaten and threatened for their bold preaching about Jesus and the new way he had taught them, they refused to back down. Their response to the threats of the 'rulers, elders, scribes and the high priest' was to call a prayer meeting and raise their voices in prayer to ask for more! [4]

---

[3] Acts 5:13, 23–32
[4] Acts 4:29–31

Several years ago I came across this definition of an apostle:

> An apostle is a messenger, someone sent on behalf of someone else, who has the power and authority of the one who sends him.[5]

In his book, *Building Churches That Last*, Dick Iverson says the classical Greek word *apostello* refers to an ambassador sent to establish a new colony, usually with a group of colonists. Applying this definition to our efforts to change the way we do church has good precedent! This is exactly what the early church did. They were forced to change the way things were done, not for the sake of change, but because their love for Jesus and their passion to tell others about him had thrust them into uncharted waters. If we are motivated to do what they did as well, there is no reason why we can't be just as radical.

Changing the way we do church has to be motivated by something greater than a dislike of the old ways. It must be apostolic in the biblical meaning of that word. We must be deeply convinced that the church has been commissioned to go into the unknown, that we have a life-changing message, good news for those who have never heard it, and that everywhere we go we are to establish outposts of the kingdom of God.

Jesus is our example of courage to bring change. Taking Jesus' life and ministry as our model helps define what it means to be apostolic. At the core, it means courage to break with the old and boldness to pioneer the new. Jesus was sent by the Father to establish the church as an outpost of heaven on earth. As *the* pioneer of our faith, Jesus was sent to show the way to the Father. He was appointed to bring a message of love to lost people, and he suffered and sacrificed to do that. He gave his life to turn the enemies of God into his friends and co-workers. He was commissioned to multiply his own life and mission on the earth by raising up and sending others.[6] Jesus paid a great price to be the

---

[5] Dick Iverson, *Building Churches That Last*, City Christian Publishing 1995, p 58.

[6] John 3:17, 34; 5:36–38; 8:42; 20:21; Matthew 28:19–20

'apostle of the faith'. He left his home, gave up his rights, lived among people as a servant, and suffered misunderstanding and rejection. There was no glamour in what Jesus did. If being an apostle means doing what Jesus did, it involves loneliness, persecution, and ultimately, death. It takes courage to follow his example.

> *Jesus paid a great price to be the 'apostle of the faith'. If being an apostle means doing what Jesus did, it involves loneliness, persecution, and ultimately death.*

The Gospel-writers describe the apostolic mission of Jesus in inspiring detail. There is an aspect to apostolic calling that is impressive in its impact on others. It's certainly a calling that is worthy of giving our lives for, if we understand it properly and our motives are right. As the apostle of our faith, Jesus had a great impact on people. He befriended outcasts from society, opposed unjust leadership structures, treated women with respect, taught public servants to be just, hung out with fringe people, and confronted the hypocrisy of sanctimonious religious leaders. It was an awesome three years – before it turned nasty. Reading about the life of Jesus as the apostle of our faith inspires me, but it also strikes fear in me. In myself, I know I'm not up to the task. I have to conclude that I can't do it on my own, but I yearn to do it nevertheless. Something in me cannot back away from the longing I have to follow the radical, awesome, noble and selfless example of Jesus.

There is a valid aspect to apostolic ministry that has to do with influencing people, even vast numbers of people, if we do it for Jesus. At some point in his life Jesus himself began to dream about a movement made up of people from every walk of life and every culture and every tribe and language. Yet, even though Jesus dreamed of a worldwide movement, he went about it in a personal, relational way. He dreamed big, but he built small. He set about changing the world, but he did it one person at a time.

We are seeking to do the same where we work in Cape Town. We have chosen to focus our efforts for now on two small townships. Our dream is to someday send hundreds of workers from these poor communities to the nations. But for now, the need is for street-level prayer and personal involvement in people's lives. It is for holistic models of church that integrate job creation for the poor with worship, and drug rehabilitation with Bible teaching. We are not the first to serve there. There are many others who have gone before us, but we see the need, and we are committed to pioneering a new way of doing church.

African believers of all cultures can teach followers of Jesus from the West much about sacrifice, overcoming injustice, and zeal for the Lord. What is often missing is a non-religious discipleship focus. Church in Africa is zealous, but has become very religious, laced with rules and traditions that are hindering the church from transforming culture.

> *To transform Africa, the church will have to change! New wineskins of church need to be created.*

Sub-Saharan Africa has been evangelized many times, but it has not been discipled. Corruption, immorality, authoritarian leadership and mistrust between tribes and races are just as prevalent in the church as in the rest of the society. The church in Africa practises passionate evangelism, but it does not do well at life-on-life discipleship. To transform Africa, the church will have to change! New wineskins of church need to be created that are filled with the new wine of changed character, changed values and changed practices. Business as usual will not cut it in Africa. The needs are too great. Wars, HIV/AIDS, corruption and sexual misconduct are a constant reminder of the need to find a new way to make a deeper impact on people's lives. I am convinced Sunday Christianity is the old way. We need a new set of beliefs and a new set of practices that emphasize every-day Christianity, not just a 'happy time on Sunday' Christianity.

As I said above, Jesus is the model for changing the old way of doing things. He broke with the Jewish ways of doing things that he himself had initiated, and if he did it to the Jews, what makes us think he will not change the church today, the very church he began 2,000 years ago? The need for a radical reformation is just as great now as it was then, much more so than is widely emphasized or taught.

For example, though he was sent by the Father to launch a worldwide movement, he spent most of his time investing in a few people, particularly marginalized and broken people. There are thousands of churches in the cities and villages of Africa, but too few of them are modelling holistic discipleship-based church like Jesus did in Palestine. The men and women Jesus spent most of his time with were not powerful, famous or recognized as leaders in his day. Jesus chose twelve ordinary men and a few women to be the first leaders of his movement. He invested in them, mentored them and taught them how to do life. His influence on them changed how the men treated their wives, how they did business in the marketplace, and how they handled their finances. He commissioned them to make more disciples like he did with them, who in turn were to raise up still others.[7] Jesus started small and personal, but he had something vast and global in mind.[8] The commission Jesus gave his first disciples reflected the greatness of the one who sent him. He worked on a personal level because the Father cares deeply for people, but he gave his

---

[7] See 2 Timothy 2:2 – Paul practised the same principle.

[8] Researchers calculate that there are more than 700 million followers of Jesus who know him personally and another 1.3 billion baptized members in traditional churches who bear his name.

disciples a worldwide commission because Father also cares for
'all nations'.[9]

Applying these lessons to my life, and the lives of those I lead,
I am determined to carry vision in my heart for all nations and for
all people, no matter what their colour or status or level of
wealth. Many times on my journey I have become discouraged.
But meditating on the example of Jesus gives me fresh courage
to carry on. I am deeply inspired by his example. Jesus started a
movement by focusing on ordinary people, not the great and the
famous.

> **Jesus started small and personal, but he
> had something vast and global in mind.**

I am convinced that being apostolic isn't limited to those people
who have the gift of apostleship. We learn from the Gospels that
Jesus wanted a movement of ordinary people to serve as his messengers.[10] Jesus announced the importance of their mission by
giving them his own title: they were also called apostles. In other
words, though Jesus appointed a few to lead with the gift of
apostleship, he called everyone who was fully devoted to him to
be *apostolic*. He wasn't setting up a hierarchy – he was mobilizing an army.

I believe all those who say yes to Jesus today receive the same
commission as the original twelve apostles. We may not all be
apostles by gifting, but we are all charged to be part of the apostolic mission of the church. If you choose to follow Jesus, you
have joined a great procession of men and women who are living
for something far greater than themselves, their jobs, their
careers or their possessions. The challenge is to act like we really
believe what we are called to be and to do. That takes courage!

---

[9] Psalm 96

[10] Acts 4:13; Matthew 4:18; 28:19–20

As a young man I came to the conclusion that if I accepted an apostolic calling, I would have God's help. I read that Jesus promised his disciples that if they obeyed his commission, he would be with them.[11] I became convinced that that command to go into all the world carried a promise that goes with it. That promise is for you and me today.[12]

He also warned the original twelve apostles that they would be persecuted, opposed and would suffer many things. We too can expect persecution and suffering if we become his messengers, his apostles. Jesus painted a picture of the great reward we would receive if we remain true to him, but he was brutally honest about the price we would have to pay to follow in his footsteps.[13]

Strong but weak

Are you called to be a pioneer? If you are like me, more times than not I have held back from taking risks for fear of failure. I have probably failed God more times than I have come through for him. I say that to make the point that to be part of an apostolic army doesn't mean you always have great courage. In fact, it is quite normal, very human of us, to be worried about what people think or say about us, or be downright terrified of suffering rejection or loss. Some of us may come across strong on the outside, but we're quite weak on the inside.

I have hung around a lot of strong leaders – you know, the ones who come across really 'anointed' when they speak in public, people who are admired as visionaries and risk-takers. But you know what? They have just as many hangs-ups as the rest of us.

---

[11] Matthew 28:20; John 20:22; Acts 1:8

[12] Jesus commanded the disciples to 'teach others also what I have commanded you' when he gave them the great commission in Matthew 28:19–20. This 'pass it on' clause makes it clear that Jesus intended the great commission to be handed down from one generation to another.

[13] Matthew 10:16–22; 16:27; John 15:18; Luke 21:16; 1 Corinthians 3:8

That's no surprise, I'm sure, but I think it's important to say. We can't hear it enough. It actually comforts me to know how human 'great' people can be. In fact, the people who don't think they have any fears or hang-ups are the people I worry about the most. They are the ones who present themselves as being together, having no problems. Those are the people that concern me.

Perhaps you don't see yourself as a courageous leader, one who takes great risks or dares to challenge the status quo. There are many faithful people in the church today who don't see themselves that way, but who are doing great things for God. Being great for God can mean getting up and going to work every day. It can mean loving your husband or wife. Doing great things for God can mean paying your bills, sharing Jesus faithfully at work, and being real with your friends. It can mean being a student and studying hard, just as Jesus did.

We know what being a courageous leader is not about. It's not about having a down line of tithers who look up to you as a great hero of the faith. It's not about having a book written about you, or a being a charismatic personality that sweeps people off their feet. What it is about is hearing from God and stepping out in faith to do the next thing God tells you to do. It's about living your life wholeheartedly for Jesus, being his man or woman. It's about saying to God that you are his messenger and by his grace you will take his message anywhere he asks you to.

Being courageous is about believing God for what he puts in your heart to do for him, and then doing it. It doesn't mean you have it all together, or that you always have faith to move mountains, but it does mean stepping out in faith to obey the next thing God tells you to do, whether you're 20 years old and have just been walking with God a few years, or you have known Christ for decades. One of the problems with not seeing ourselves as courageous is that we don't take up the challenges God has for us. We excuse ourselves, let ourselves 'off the hook' so to speak. If we say we are going to courageously follow Jesus, then we are, on record, accountable to live that way.

> *Being a courageous leader is about believing God for what he puts in your heart to do for him, and then doing it.*

After searching to find out my calling as a young man, and then discovering that I was called to risk-taking leadership, and living that way for more than 40 years, I can now say that I am determined to end my life more passionate than I began it. I want to finish on fire, more fiercely focused on following Jesus and living for his purposes on the earth than I was when I was 20 years old and trying to figure out what my ministry was going to be. By the way, I have discovered that God is more concerned about my passion than my ministry. I have learned that if I keep my heart on fire for him, he will take care of my ministry.

I am passionate. I dream about the nations being won for Christ. But now I have the advantage of a lifetime of service to the Lord. As a father in the Lord, my dream now is to raise up sons and daughters in the Lord, who in turn will have their own spiritual sons and daughters.

That is why Sally and I have moved to Cape Town. We are pouring our lives into the next generation of risk-takers. We call our training CPx – referring to a 'church-planting experience'. For those who want to learn a new way of living out their faith among the poor and disenfranchised and unreached, we give them an opportunity to learn, first hand. We walk side by side with those who join us to help them start small, simple, easily reproducible communities made up of people they share Jesus with and help practically. We do it first here in Cape Town, but our aim is to send workers to *all nations*.

We help people learn how to re-imagine church, then experiment with how to do it as a simple, joyful community that encourages everyone involved to use their passions and gifts to reach out to others. We are working on finding simple ways of doing church that are holistic, sustainable and reproducible. We make mistakes, but we are having fun!

Becoming an apostolic people

Being apostolic is about a pioneering spirit, about believing God for new things no matter what season of life you're in. I am over 60 years old and Sally is not far behind. Most of the people in our age bracket are planning their retirement. We are starting out on a new assignment.[14]

Taking this step has led me to reflect on my earlier longings to know my ministry. It has reminded me of my desperation as a young man to hear from God, to know his direction for my life. I discovered early on that if I am serious with God, he will hear my cry and respond. I know we can't make demands of God, but we can grieve over what we don't have, and fast and pray with desperation for what we long to have, from God. If we cry out to God, he promises he will hear our cry and answer us.

We are told that God heard the cry of his people when they were in Egypt's bondage in Exodus 3:7. He also heard the cry of Hannah (1 Samuel 1:10), David (2 Samuel 22:7; 1 Kings 8:28) and Mordecai (Esther 4:1). Jeremiah 33:3 promises that if we call out to him, he will hear us and answer us. Deuteronomy 4:29 says we must cry to him with all our hearts. God longs for us to be desperate for him.

---

[14] Visit our personal website – www.floydandsally.org – to learn more about how you can be part of what we are doing in South Africa and other nations around the world. You can also visit our ministry website – www.all-nations.info – to find out more about All Nations.

The search continues

When Sally and I stepped out in faith and pioneered the simple-church movement we call 'All Nations', we were taking up a call I received from God when we were newly married. I was 21, and we were staying in a pastor's home in upstate New York. We were travelling and speaking in local churches to recruit workers for short-term outreaches. I was reading a book one day when I had an unexpected encounter with God. I was reading about the life of General Douglas MacArthur. The book was titled *American Caesar* (written by William Manchester). MacArthur led the American forces in the Pacific theatre during World War Two. Putting to one side his issues of personal pride, I was very inspired by his gifts as a strategic thinker and planner, and how well he prepared his men for battle. I learned that he lost fewer men during the years he led the American forces in the Pacific theatre than were lost in just one battle in Europe (the Battle of the Bulge, where the Americans suffered some 75,000 casualties).

I lifted a silent prayer as I read the book, telling God that I wanted to do the same as MacArthur, except for his army. I told him I wanted to mobilize and train an army of men and women for him. I wanted to prepare them for battle, to equip and coach them to be wise warriors for God. I didn't realize it then, but I was signing up for the army we read about in Ezekiel 37.

As I was reading the book, suddenly I saw in my mind's eye teams of people going to the continents of the world. I saw them preaching and making disciples, and I saw them being equipped to serve God before they went out. I felt God's Spirit move on my heart. I wept with joy and excitement and hope for what I saw. I had to pray. I got on my knees beside the couch I was sitting on.

Suddenly I saw in my mind's eye teams of people going to the continents of the world.

That experience was a turning point for me. It impacted me so deeply that every decision I made from then on was made in the light of that experience. Everything I did was to help fulfil the picture God gave me of mobilizing an army of men and women who would serve God in the nations. It stayed with me for the rest of my life. When I would get discouraged, when I would question my direction, I would go back to the time God spoke to me, to the picture he gave me. From that time on I burned with desire to see people won to Jesus in the nations.

Years later, when Sally and I were praying once again about our direction, I remembered what God said to me as a young man. We were very discouraged. I was going for long walks, praying and reflecting on the isolation we felt, and the longing I had for a fresh word from the Lord. I have discovered that even when I am surrounded with people who love me, I can still feel isolated and alone. It was like that for Sally and me. We were leading a wonderful ministry, had great friends, lived in a beautiful place, yet something was missing. I have learned that these times are arranged by God for us to seek *him*. It's his way of putting desperation in our hearts for him, to prepare us for the fresh word he wants to give us. These types of experiences usually precede a major decision in our lives. As I said, it's God's way of preparing us, of stirring our hearts to be alone with him so we can hear his voice.

During that time, it seemed that every time I picked up the Bible, verses about the nations jumped off the page. Repeatedly, God gave me passages with the words 'all nations' or 'all peoples' in them. I started dreaming about what more we could do to plant churches in the nations. Then one morning, during a time of prayer and meditation in Psalm 96, I read these words: '. . .declare his glory among the nations, his wonders among *all peoples*. . . .' That was the third or fourth time in a few days that the phrase 'all nations' jumped out from the page to me. While I was reading, I received a telephone call from one of our co-workers. 'Can you come over and join the students for the worship time this morning, Floyd? There's a lady here, she's the real deal, and she feels she has a word for you.' Cautiously, I agreed.

The lady turned out to be someone I knew and trusted, and with tears she shared her word with me. It was Psalm 96, the same passage I was reading earlier that morning! She encouraged me that what the Lord had been saying to me was from him. I knew that God was calling me to step out in faith. God was calling me to once again claim the promise he had given to me as a 21-year-old. He was stirring me to believe him for teams of young people to go to each continent, to preach and make disciples among 'all nations'.

Our journey has taken some strange twists since that time, but God has been with us each step of the way. Today, the ministry we call 'All Nations' has helped mobilize and send teams all over the world. Every year, students attend CPx, the live-learn discipleship and discipleship-training programme run under the auspices of All Nations.

What does courageous leadership look like in your life?

When you inspire your friends and people around you to obey the commands of Jesus, and you model obedience to Jesus yourself, you are courageous. When you go one step further and intentionally invest in the lives of those you are discipling to obey the great commission, you are equipping them for courageous ministry. The word 'equip' is used by Paul in Ephesians 4:12. It was originally a medical term used to describe what happens when a broken limb is mended and set straight. To equip someone one is to mend what is broken in their life so they can go all out for Jesus.

Being courageous is about inspiring others to partner with God in his mission on planet earth. We join his mission by living a lifestyle of personal evangelism, prayer, and disciple-making, and by inviting others to do the same. Apostolic people have stories to tell. They inspire others to believe God to use them to make a difference in the world. It is through courageous, apostolic people that God spurs the church to reach people with the good news about Jesus.

Courageous leaders mobilize courageous people

When we lose the vision for why God has put us on the earth, we need leaders who will speak for God, who will remind us that we are here for God and his purposes. Reaching out to the unchurched and poor of the earth is central to God's purpose for the church and for each of our lives. To use a biblical phrase, we are called 'outside the gate.'[15] When Jesus was crucified, he was led outside the gates of Jerusalem. Apostolic people follow Jesus' example and go outside the gates. We go where we are not comfortable. We take risks. We get away from comfortable and familiar church life and get among the people.

Apostolic people can do this in any one of a number of vocations. It doesn't matter what their place of employment. People in the marketplace are just as called by God as those called to reach lost tribes in the Amazon. Like Jesus when he worked as a carpenter, some are called to ordinary jobs. The fact that Jesus served for eighteen years as a carpenter is intended by God to be an example to those in the marketplace. They are just as called and commissioned to minister within their vocation as those who go to other nations. By working as a carpenter, Jesus was modelling how he wants the church to infiltrate every sphere of life.

The strategy Jesus followed in the next season of life, the three years of intentional discipleship with the twelve, modelled the goals and methods we should follow no matter what vocation God has called us to. In the two seasons of his life, Jesus both

---

[15] Hebrews 13:12

validated the sanctity of ordinary life, and modelled how to intentionally make disciples as we do 'ordinary' life.

Crossing the seas doesn't make one missional, but living purposefully for God does.

To be dedicated to Jesus is not first of all about being a missionary or pastor, but being intentional and obedient in making disciples. You can be a pastor who is not dedicated, and you can be an engineer who is sold out to God. To join God's mission is not about geography or vocation, but passionate obedience. Crossing the seas doesn't make one missional, but living purposefully for God does. We are called to be full-time, whether it be in Canterbury or Canberra, whether as an accountant or a relief worker. We are all called to follow Jesus by making disciples who also love and obey Jesus.

Apostolic men and women are given authority by God to lead the church to do what Jesus did when he was here on earth. They are sent as messengers to people who don't know Jesus, and they are called to inspire and equip others to do the same. They do this by following Jesus' example: by making and gathering disciples of Jesus. Apostolic people take the church to the world, they don't wait for the world to come to the church. God always intends the fruit of apostolic service to result in more obedient disciples for Jesus. That means getting them together in small, simple gatherings, then equipping and encouraging them to obey all Jesus taught us to do. When the Holy Spirit falls on such a missional community and it begins to grow out of control, a church-planting movement is born.

Apostolic people take the church to the world, they don't wait for the world to come to the church.

God uses those who are gifted as apostles to mobilize the whole church to be apostolic. God has wired apostles with a restlessness and dissatisfaction with the ordinary that is only satisfied when they boldly reach the lost – and motivate others to do the same. They are not supposed to be satisfied with the status quo. Their calling is to look over the horizon to those places where the church has not yet gone, and go there. While others see what has been done and are grateful, apostolic people see what has not been done and long for more.

Without its apostles, the church becomes hopelessly ingrown, and ultimately disobedient to Jesus' commission to disciple all nations. When local churches, Christian organizations and educational institutions marginalize or exclude those with apostolic passion, they can no longer expect to be fully obedient to Jesus.

> When local churches, Christian organizations and educational institutions marginalize or exclude those with apostolic passion, they can no longer expect to be fully obedient to Jesus.

Caution: danger ahead

True to their passion, courageous, apostolic leaders constantly look over the horizon, searching for new challenges. But they must be cautious. They have to learn to exercise discernment to go with their zeal. They cannot afford to jump on the bandwagon of every new thing that comes to town, or every fresh vision that comes to mind. The visionary capacity within apostolic leaders enables them to see new vision. But the danger of unfocused vision is just that: a lack of consistent focus on the one thing they are called to do above all others.

Effective apostolic leaders have learned they can waste their time blessing many things without building one thing well.

Apostolic leaders are called to work with others in a spirit of unity, but they are not called to run from one unity conference to another, looking for the newest and latest 'word from the Lord'. They are called to 'think apostolically' as they listen prophetically. They are called to bless what other genuine followers of Jesus do for him, but they are called to build what God has given them to do and focus on reaching the lost. They are called to bless others, but not to lead a 'blessing' ministry. They are called to partner with others, but not to sacrifice their pioneering anointing. They are called to build. Effective apostolic leaders have learned they can waste their time blessing many things without building one thing well. Apostolic leaders are called to focus their gifts and energies, and the gifts and energies of those they lead, on winning, maturing and multiplying others in church-planting movements. They can do this in the marketplace and in the nations. If they do this well, they are 'wise master builders.'[16] Not to do so is to be a foolish builder.

If you are devoted to apostolic ministry, and gathering and multiplying new disciples for Jesus does not excite you, there is a good chance you need to go back to the cross. You may need to fall in love with Jesus all over again, to catch a fresh vision of why God made you the way he did. Effective disciples of Jesus know what they are called to do, and they do it single-mindedly. It's certainly not for their own entertainment or fulfilment that they are called to follow Jesus. They are not gifted with the gifts God has given them to bounce from one visionary endeavour to another. They are called to build God's church – no matter what their vocation in life. Apostolic people are passionate for Jesus and his

---

[16] 1 Corinthians 3:10

purposes on the earth. They are called by Jesus to build, and builders are called to build the church. If you're one of those people, and you have lost that vision, or never had it in the first place, you may not be fulfilling your destiny in God.

Courageous people I know

It may help to realize that the Spirit may call some of us to apostolic activity though we are not apostles by gifting. He may call us to pioneer a new ministry or to plant a church, though pioneering may not be the norm for our lives. Paul describes this to the Corinthian church as 'diversities of activities':

> There are diversities of gifts, but the same Spirit. There are differences of ministries, but the same Lord. And there are *diversities of activities*, but it is the same God who works all in all.[17]

Paul reminds us in this verse that God gives different ministries and different activities to different people to spread the gospel and build his church.[18] If you are called upon by God to be part of a church-planting or pioneering endeavour, it is helpful if you are linked with those who have an apostolic gift. If you are part of a church or movement that has developed an apostolic culture, all the better.

> While all apostles today have the gift of an apostle, not all those who are given apostolic assignments have an apostolic gift.

Confusion concerning the term 'apostle' arises when we don't make a distinction between the first apostles, apostolic assignments

---

[17] 1 Corinthians 12:4–6

[18] Acts 1:25; 13:1–3; Romans 1:5; 16:7; Galatians 2:8; 2 Timothy 1:11

that can be given to anyone, and those individuals who have been given the gift of apostleship in the church today. To summarize:

○ *the first apostles* – the ones who saw the resurrected Jesus and were called to pioneer the church in its first season of existence
○ *apostolic assignments* – given to anyone the Holy Spirit chooses, to do the same thing the early church apostles did
○ *the gift of apostleship* – given to individuals in the church today to win, gather and multiply followers of Jesus

The first twelve apostles who were with Jesus in the flesh were also apostles by gifting. They were unique in that they saw Jesus in his resurrected body, and received the great commission the first time it was given. Paul also received this same office and status because of his personal encounter with Christ on the road to Damascus. Paul saw Jesus in his resurrection glory, and it blinded him. During this encounter, Jesus commissioned Paul just as he did the other apostles who were with him.[19]

One of the clearest examples in my experience of God using someone who is not an apostle for apostolic activity is the story of Lura Garrido. God used Lura to plant churches among prostitutes in Amsterdam's infamous red light district. Lura was working for me at the time as a personal assistant. Lura asked me for a half-day off each week to do evangelism among the prostitutes. I happily agreed, thinking how wonderful it was that one of our office workers wanted to spend more time telling people about Jesus. It wasn't long before she asked for another half-day off, and then another full day away from the office. I followed Lura's activities closely, and was amazed how God used this tiny, 62-year-old woman to win and disciple scores of street girls to himself.

Lura started a Bible study group for former prostitutes that grew to over 150 converts. Today there are more than 800 people

---

[19] Acts 9:3 ff.

in the church begun by Lura, including congregations worshipping in four different languages. When I told her she was pastoring a church, not just leading a Bible study group, she laughed and told me she wasn't a pastor. And in the traditional sense of the word, she was right. In terms of spiritual gifts, Lura was a teacher/evangelist who loved women from the streets.

The work Lura began spread to other cities, and it wasn't long before my sweet, grandmotherly assistant was a circuit-riding, church-planting 'apostle' to the prostitutes of Holland. That was many years ago, and Lura is still involved in ministry to the women of the red light district. She is in her late seventies now. Who says God can't use women to plant churches? And who says God can't use any person he chooses to accomplish an apostolic assignment for him?

Lura's assignment was long-term and far-reaching. The reason I call it an assignment rather than a gifting is simply this: Lura was not an apostle in the way the term is commonly used today, nor was she called or equipped to plant churches outside of this, her specific area of ministry.

There are others I could tell you about in our little movement whose courage inspires me: David and Anna and their market-place project in India; Mike and Domnica's stories about the youth church in Romania always get me smiling; Bill and Norren and Babu Kaji and Goma have given up everything to pioneer a holistic church-planting ministry among the poor in Kathmandu; Bob and Sonam and Maika and Heather will quickly tell you the real heroes of their work are the Buddhist and Hindu converts and their amazing child-like faith; Blake and Tracy have deeply impacted me with their perseverance and prayer life and how that has led to fresh revelation concerning the Ancient One and his love for the Akha people.

I am convinced that it is not the famous but the faithful who will receive the big crowns in heaven. Like Bill and Julie Ross and the simple-church community they have launched in South

Dakota on Julie's mother's farm. And Mark and Sarah Rife and the Elevate community in Hilo, Hawaii. They will be the first to tell you pioneering is not easy, and sometimes it is courage alone that keeps them going.

Walter Snyman is also one of my heroes of courage. Pastor Walter opened the doors to the Lighthouse Church in Cape Town to people of all colours and cultures in 1982, long before it was the politically correct thing to do. Now his son, Peter, and other emerging leaders at the Lighthouse are following in the footsteps of Pastor Walter and his wife, Colleen, in terms of courage. Now their gaze is on becoming an apostolic movement of simple churches that touch the nations for Jesus.

Ten characteristics of courageous apostolic people

- *Vision.* Apostolic people see things other people don't see. They tend to live in the future, thinking about the next mountain to climb. Never tell these people something is impossible: it motivates them to want to be the first to do it!
- *Faith.* Apostolic people believe God for the unattainable. The Holy Spirit gives them faith to attempt the impossible.
- *Building, not just blessing.* Apostolic people get things done. They establish new works, plant new churches, start new businesses, and gather and unite people around a shared vision and common values.
- *Miraculous supply.* The Spirit blesses them with miracles and many other signs and wonders. It is God's goodness to them to encourage them as they reach the neglected and unreached peoples of the earth.
- *Starting new churches.* Apostolic people are gatherers of people. The purpose of apostolic ministry is to attract those who don't follow Jesus so new churches will be planted and the worship of Jesus spread to more people and places.
- *Settle disputes and apply discipline.* Those who do apostolic

ministry are called on to settle disputes among co-workers and apply church discipline when needed. Authority is given to them by God to establish healthy, reproducing congregations. The purpose of church discipline is to restore those who are fallen and keep the church pure and focused in its mission to spread the gospel.

○ *Appoint and coach local church leaders.* Paul appointed elders in the churches he planted on his missionary journeys. The purpose of apostolic ministry is to help spread the gospel through planting self-multiplying, self-propagating and self-sustaining churches.

○ *Suffer persecution and endure hardship.* One of the consequences of apostolic ministry is to break open closed countries or territories and pioneer new beachheads for the gospel. Because of the pioneering nature of their calling, apostolic people experience misunderstanding, rejection and persecution. The more hostile the beliefs of those being reached the greater the chance of persecution.

○ *Impart values and vision.* Courageous leaders empower the people of God to stay focused on their calling by casting a compelling vision and imparting kingdom values.

○ *Movements and networks.* Paul networked churches together (Ephesus, Colosse, Laodicea in one grouping, the house churches in Rome in another). He did this in order to facilitate the spread of the gospel and to build unity among the believers.[20] Many apostolic leaders today have begun to employ this biblical strategy by starting loosely affiliated church-planting movements that mobilize churches to reach more people with the gospel. Movements *move* people!

---

[20] See Romans 15:7

Courageous leaders are developed in the furnace of opposition

There is increasing cynicism towards visionary leaders in modern society. In fact, you don't have to be a cynic to be sceptical when someone proclaims a big vision. Most people have heard at least one leader spin a vision of how they are going to change the world. Even if you believe the world needs changing, and believe God is going to change it someday, it is still difficult to whole-heartedly trust a leader when he or she casts a daring vision.

Daunting as the challenge may be, this is what leadership is all about. Leading reluctant people and helping them overcome their objections and fears is what helps leaders stay close to God – and learn vital leadership competencies. If spiritual leaders face these challenges with humility, their responses will gain them credibility and influence. Spiritual authority can never be sepa-rated from the ability to influence people in a non-manipulative way. Leading is serving, serving gives influence, and influence yields the fruit of true spiritual authority.

> *Leading reluctant people and helping them overcome their objections and fears is what helps leaders stay close to God.*

One purpose above all others

God has given visionary leaders to the church for one purpose above all others: to see, to savour and to spread the glory of God in every neighbourhood, every sphere of society, and every nation in the earth. If the chief end of man is to glorify God and enjoy him for ever, the chief end of courageous leaders is to lead God's people into seeing, savouring and spreading the glory of God. He has placed them in the church to magnify and intensify God's fiery desire to display his glory in and through his people.

God gave leaders to the church to spread his glory, not to be seen as glorious in the eyes of people.

Apostleship is not the 'top rung' of leadership achievement in the church; God's glory is ultimate. Being a courageous leader is not about notoriety; it is about God and his glory. Courageous leadership is a means to an end. Spiritual leadership will someday pass away, but the beauty and radiance of his glory will abide for ever. God gave leaders to the church to spread his glory, not to be seen as glorious in the eyes of people.

Being a courageous leader is about being a messenger. It is the glory of the message we carry, not the fancy footwork of the messenger as we march on the journey that is to inspire the church. When we reach the end of the age, and we join the redeemed from every tribe and people and tongue and nation, and fall on our faces and worship the Lamb who is worthy, who will notice that leadership as we know it is no more? It is a temporary grace. The Lamb is for ever.

The glory of God is ultimate, not the gifts God has given to spread his glory. When this age is over, and we bow in his presence, true apostles will long for one thing, and that is to look into his eyes and see the pleasure and joy Jesus receives when there is more worship offered up to him. That's what true apostles strive for: to enjoy Jesus and the delight he has when we bring him more worship through discipling more worshippers. Our ultimate goal is not how many churches we have planted, or leaders we have trained, or businesses we have started. This is our dream: at the end of time, to be able to look into those beautiful, piercing eyes and know that we have pleased him, that he is worshipped and enjoyed and loved by those we have brought to him. That is our reward. That is enough. We ask no more than that.

This is the crown all true leaders want to lay at his feet. You have a choice about this, dear friend: at the end of time you can stand before God with empty hands, or you can come to him with crowns to lay before him. You cannot bring your books, CDs, radio programmes, or any human achievement to lay at his feet. It is redeemed people he longs for. Those are the crowns we lay before him. The ultimate prize of every courageous leader is not what rewards he or she receives on earth, but the reward the Lamb receives in heaven. Paul said,

> For what is our hope, or joy, or crown of rejoicing? Is it not even you in the presence of our Lord Jesus Christ. . .?[21]

The glory God receives through the worship of the redeemed is both the fuel and the goal of courageous leaders. It's the fuel because it is what empowers all pioneers of the faith to press on. We long to see the Lamb receive the just reward of his suffering. It is our goal because the work of leading and pioneering has but one ultimate goal, and that is the pleasure and joy of bringing the poor and the lost into the experience of his mercy and goodness. The enjoyment of the Lamb for ever by those we have yet to reach with the good news is what moves and motivates us:

> Thou art worthy, O Lord, to receive glory and honour and power: for thou hast created all things, and for thy pleasure they are and were created.[22]

As John Piper has reminded us, the savouring of God in private worship precedes the proclaiming of God in public service. We can't commend what we don't treasure ourselves. Apostolic leaders will never cry from the depths of their being, 'Worthy is the Lamb', who have not seen him and savoured him alone in the secret place.

> If the pursuit of *God's* glory is not ordered above the pursuit of *man's* good in the affections of the heart and the priorities of the church, man will not be well served and God will not be duly honoured. . .[23]

---

[21] 1 Thessalonians 2:19, KJV   [22] Revelation 4:11, KJV

[23] John Piper, *Let the Nations Be Glad*, IVP 2003

Distracted leaders?

As I said at the close of the last chapter, when I was younger I desperately wanted to know my ministry, and perhaps that was the problem: I wanted to know *my* ministry. I was in danger of being distracted from the main thing: living for God, not myself. Being preoccupied with finding 'my ministry' or 'my calling', no matter how natural that may seem, can be a dangerous distraction. It's quite likely that we who serve the church can end up being distracted from the God we love if we are not daily seeing and savouring God's glory. When Moses was at the end of himself as a leader, he cried out, 'Show me your glory!'[24] If your courage has faded or your passion has dried up, there is only one place to go, and that is the secret place with God, alone. Even now, stop and get on your knees, and ask him for a fresh revelation of his glory, a deeper revelation of his beauty as revealed in Christ Jesus.

When we lose sight of his glory, the message of God's greatness is diminished in our eyes, and in the eyes of those we lead. When this is the case, we make God look small and unimpressive, like a limited God who is anxious about the ultimate outcome of his enterprise. How we experience him alone in his presence is how we will present him to others in public.

Courageous leadership is birthed and nurtured out of a fresh revelation of God in the person of Jesus. Moses encountered God in the wilderness. Abraham met him at the altar of sacrifice. David met him in the hill country of Palestine on the run from Saul. Paul met him on the road to Damascus. How long has it been since you saw his glory? Moses pledged he would not go forward if God's presence did not go with him. Will you pledge the same? Right now? I appeal to you to kneel before the Father of heaven and earth and pledge to him that you will not represent him to others if you do not see him for yourself. Promise God

---

[24] Exodus 33:18

you will not do the work of ministry without being in his presence daily, seeking his face and reading his word. Then you will see him with new eyes. And you will see the way forward with courage in your heart.

PART THREE
Focused Obedience

5

Watch Out for the Camels

It's not easy to miss a camel in the middle of the road, but there we were, chugging down the highway and it ran right out in front of us. It was dusk, the sun was setting over the Hindu Kush Mountains, and we were relieved to finally be on our way. It had taken us weeks to fix up the old Austrian touring bus we bought from a young tourist. It was outfitted as a hippy home on wheels, with bunk beds, shower and all. Not very fancy, but we loved it. We loaded all our worldly possessions onto it, hugged everyone in sight, tucked in our newly born daughter, Misha, and were on our way.

We had lived in Kabul in Afghanistan for almost three years, running our half-way house for Western drop-outs. But now the Afghan government had changed hands and the hardliners decided to send us packing. No more visas for helping the so-called decadent youth of the West. From their point of view, it was tough luck if you got caught with drugs or lost your money. They didn't want us there to help people out of their problems.

It was sad to leave the land we had grown to love, even though we didn't fit in with our long hair and unconventional ways of doing things. Afghanistan was a barren, mountainous land; one of the poorest in the world. But Afghans are known for their generous hospitality, and the people were friendly once they figured out we were not a threat to them.

But it was time to leave. We packed our bus and headed out. Not long after we cleared the outskirts of Kabul, I noticed a band of Bedouin-type nomads camping in the fields on the side of the road. I slowed down for one last look at these hardy people who moved from one mountain valley to another before heading to Kabul each year for the annual camel auction. A Bedouin man's wealth was measured in camels, not cash.

There were hundreds of Bedouins living in black tents alongside the road, arranged by families. Sheep and camels were everywhere. I was trying to keep one eye on the road and at the same time get a good look at the camel herds. Camels are fascinating animals; ugly if you look them in the eye, but hearty burden-bearers and fun to watch. I was also trying to catch a glimpse of the men herding the camels, dressed in long shirts that hung down to their knees covering baggy pants that billowed in the wind.

I noticed one lone camel stray from the herd and start across the road, just 100 metres in front of us. I slowed down, when suddenly a huge oil tanker flew past me going at least 70 miles an hour. I hit the breaks, hoping the truck driver could see the camel now standing in the middle of the highway.

I hit the breaks, hoping the truck driver could see the camel now standing in the middle of the highway.

The driver was looking at me, gesticulating to me to get out of his way, no doubt frustrated that I was driving so slowly. The drivers of these huge tankers hauling oil to Kabul from Iran were notorious for their reckless, high-speed driving.

Then he slammed into the camel! The poor beast didn't stand a chance. The truck levelled the camel, killing it instantly. I slowed down and pulled around the hairy beast lying on the road. The driver jumped out of his big, shiny oil tanker and chased our bus down the road, waving a tyre iron, yelling for us to stop. It was chaos. Bedouin women were ululating and a posse of very unhappy men came running from their tents. One of my last memories of Afghanistan is looking in my side-view mirror, watching that burly Iranian truck driver pointing at us, yelling and screaming at a crowd of Bedouins gathered around their dead camel!

There was no way I was going to stop and try and explain my version of things. The last thing I wanted to do was spend time in an Afghan prison, taking the rap for the reckless Iranian truck driver. A long-haired hippy was always going to be the bad guy in that scenario. The camel was worth one year's wages in local currency – money we didn't have to spare.

The memory of that camel getting creamed, the sudden rush of adrenaline and fear, and the dread of getting thrown in prison kept me focused on the road. Don't you know I kept my eyes glued to the road the rest of the 5,000-mile journey? I was determined to get to my destination, and when you are desperate, you stay focused.

When you are desperate, you stay focused.

Staying focused was a challenge for me when I was growing up. My attention span is not that great. I was always looking for a new adventure. My mother had to practically chain me to my desk to get me to do my homework. As an adult, one of the things I dread most is boredom. The discipline of sticking with something until it is finished and finished well is a character trait that has not come naturally to me. I love variety and am constantly looking for new things to do.

Being wired this way is not all bad, of course. God made me to love change, to enjoy learning new things. He created me with a sense of adventure. I love the challenge of conquering a new skill or discovering something about life I never knew before. In fact, it's part of my spiritual gift mix. I am visionary by nature. I dream about doing new things for God. I see needs all around me and get three or four ideas a day about how to meet those needs. The hard part for me is not seeing new things to do – the hard part is sticking with something once I have started it.

I am not saying this about myself because I feel inferior to others. I am saying it because I have met leaders all over the world who face the same challenge. The issue of focus applies to all our lives. Dreamer or no dreamer, we are called to be faithful to the purposes of God. If you are not a visionary leader, your life is most likely affected by one.

Some visionary leaders understand how God has made them and have developed the skills and character strengths to enable them to live lives of focused obedience. Others flounder because they keep changing their vision. The vision becomes an end in itself, rather than a means to obey the last commandment of Jesus: go, teach, baptize and make disciples.[1]

Three ways to learn faithfulness

Staying focused is not just a challenge for visionary leaders. Another way to describe focus is faithfulness. Faithfulness – what my dad used to call 'stick-to-it-iveness' – is a quality all of us need to work on. Being what the Bible calls a 'faithful servant' is an essential trait to please God and do what he calls us to do. Jesus promised that the person who is faithful in little will become 'lord over much'.[2] In the same passage, Jesus taught that the servant who is faithful over mammon – things – would earn the right to be a steward of spiritual matters. In other words, if you don't pay your bills and don't keep your word, professing readiness to obey God is just so much hype. God can't trust a person with spiritual treasures who is not faithful in the practical issues of life.

---

[1] Matthew 28:19–20   [2] Luke 16:10–12

Another way to describe focus is faithfulness. God can't trust a person who is not faithful.

Jesus taught in the same passage that a person who has not learned to be faithful in 'another man's vineyard' will not be master of his own. What Jesus meant by this was that learning to serve another person's vision or ministry, learning to be faithful in our service under someone else's leadership, is a prerequisite for being trusted by God to lead others. Serving people teaches us lessons that prepare us for finding our place in the kingdom of God.

Watch out for big hairy camels

'Watch out for the camels' is another way of saying how important it is to be faithful, to stick with something. There are distractions in life, many of them appealing. But it is the woman or man who knows what God has given them to do in life and remains focused on that who will receive a reward at the end of life.

It may help to define what it means to be a focused person. It means to give a determined, concentrated effort and your full attention to the particular thing God has called you to, such as an assigned responsibility or a commitment to do something. Focus is the ability to concentrate, to give your unqualified attention to what you are called to do and be. It is the quality of clear and relentless determination. It means sticking with something until it is finished.

A focused person can see a need and stay focused on what they see. They have a sharp, defined focal point. Focus is not just about what we see outside ourselves. A focused person has a fixed point of reference in terms of their core values and standards as well. They have inner strength. Some people may think a focused person is stubborn. I think of that person as reliable.

They know what they are called to do in life and they stay with it. They can be counted on. They don't change their message or behaviour to please the crowd they are with.

A focused person is not moved by lack of approval. They have deep inner convictions that allow them to give their attention to the one thing they are assigned by God. Jesus focused on the cross. He would not be deterred from going up to Jerusalem at the time that was appointed to him to die – by his friends or his enemies. Paul was a man of single focus. He spoke to the Philippians of 'this *one* thing I do. . .'.[3] David wrote in the Psalms, '*one* thing I desired of the Lord. . .'.[4]

A focused person is not moved by lack of approval.

Notice the steel in Paul's spirit, the determination and focus of his commitment reflected in these words spoken to elders of the church in Ephesus at the end of his life:

> But none of these things move me; nor do I count my life dear to myself, so that I may finish my race with joy, and the ministry which I received from the Lord Jesus, to testify to the gospel of the grace of God. [5]

To focus is to adjust your vision so that you see clearly and sharply. We speak about focusing a camera lens. To be focused is not something that happens to us, it is what we do. It is a verb, an action we undertake. Focus is the result of spiritual concentration, of choosing and nurturing the values and vision God has given us. I have known a few people who had no sense of alignment of their values and vision. When such a person, or a movement of persons, has clearly aligned values and vision, their lives and energy can be illustrated like this:

---

[3] Philippians 3:13

[4] Psalm 27:4   [5] Acts 20:24

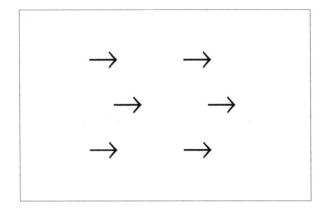

When our values and vision are not focused, it looks like this:

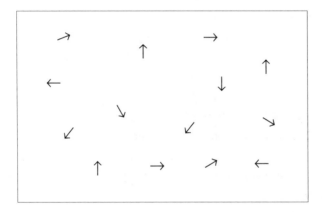

We are energized when we have congruent values and vision. That is what gives us the power to 'stick with it'. Focus is what allows us to stay the course, to finish the journey. Without focus we lose sight of the destination. An unfocused vision results in taking the side-roads of life and then calling them the main road.

Notice what Paul said: 'None of these things move me. . .' What are the things that he would not allow to move him? In the context Paul was speaking in, it was threats to his life, imprisonment, abandonment by friends and accusations of enemies. Suffering and hardship awaited him if he carried on his journey to Jerusalem. That's what the prophets told him and the Spirit bore witness in his own heart. But Paul carried on, determined to stick by the values and vision that guided his life. Paul did not make his decisions based on consequences but beliefs in what was right.

An unfocused vision results in taking the side-roads of life and then calling them the main road.

It doesn't take much to get sidetracked in life. Think about how fragmented modern life is. We are pulled in different directions by naturally being involved in different circles of relationships: people we work with, neighbours, church friends, family, parents and family members of those in school, sports and recreation acquaintances and more. Then there is the time it takes to drive to work. If we are going to build our lives in authentic friendships with a few others in simple church, we will have to say no, no, no. If you are passionate about engaging your culture with others in organic church, you will have to say no to many good things in life. You will have to reduce the 'circles' in your life, the spheres of activity that draw you away from faithfulness to what you believe in and are committed to. Simple church requires us to simplify life.

Modernization with all its advantages also has disadvantages that can cause us to live a fragmented and harried existence. We normally live at a hectic, speedy pace that mitigates against what organic church, the *ecclesia*, is called to be. You don't have to consciously say yes to sin and temptations to be compromised by our modern way of life, just go with the flow. Do what is expected of you, and you lose the battle for focused obedience.

Knowing where we are headed and going there with fierce determination is the quality of a person who can be counted on. That person lives a focused life. It is what allows us to finish well. Focus keeps us on the journey with clear vision. Many a person has ended up confused and disappointed because they lost sight of the goal, of the destination. It is easy to be distracted. There are many tempting stops and detours along the way.

In this chapter I will share some of the causes of distraction; what I call the camels in the road. These are the things that keep us from staying focused on the main thing. Do you know the main thing in your life and are you focused on it?

When Paul said, 'None of these things move me. . .',[6] he was referring to the things that could have kept him from obeying the call of God on his life. We all have a calling, and we all face tempting distractions from 'things that move' us. There are 'things' in life, the camels, whether they are big or little, that by their nature *can* move us if we let them. I mentioned two big ones just above: the busyness of life and the fragmented nature of modern lifestyle. Other distractions that can 'move' us include betrayal of a friend, family tragedies, an opportunity of a lifetime to make a ton of money, loss of a job or a demotion at work, divorce, or conflict with someone we love are all part of the 'things' of life that can and do 'move' us. These are the circumstances in life that the enemy seeks to use to 'take us out'.

God's desire for each of us is to bring us to a place of trust in his character that enables us to receive his grace to overcome the trials and testings we go through, and to resist the luring temptations we face, so we remain fiercely determined to gain the prize God sets before us. In describing the shipwrecks, beatings, imprisonments, personal attacks, and physical hardships of life, Paul said he was 'under a sentence of death. . .'. Serving the Lord as a leader or worker in the church can be one of those trials – it often is for spiritual leaders. But Paul saw the difficult circumstances he went through as from God. He understood that God did not cause the distractions he faced, but he believed God was using them.

Listen again to what Paul said about the purpose of the 'sentence of death' he was under:

---

[6] Acts 20:24

> Yes, we had the sentence of death in ourselves, but that was so we should not trust in ourselves but in God who raises the dead. . .[7]

Here's how Eugene Peterson translates this verse:

> We felt like we'd been sent to death row, that it was all over for us. As it turned out, it was the best thing that could have happened. Instead of trusting in our own strength or wits to get out of it, we were *forced to trust God totally*—not a bad idea since he's the God who raises the dead![8]

Paul said he was 'forced to trust God.' *Forced* to trust God? Have you ever felt backed into a corner by God? God does lead us into situations like that but we always have a choice. It's not a choice of getting out of the corner. The choice God gives us in times like that is to trust him or not to trust him. There is always grace available to trust God but it is a choice if we will take hold of that grace and say yes to living more simply, to cutting out commitments that keep us running in circles, moving to a smaller home with a smaller house payment, and living closely with a few friends so we can engage the world together. A little later in his letter to the Corinthians, after telling them he was under a sentence of death, Paul told them not to squander the grace of God.[9] He said,

> We beg you, please don't squander one bit of this marvelous life God has given us. God reminds us, "I heard your call in the nick of time; The day you needed me, I was there to help."

There is grace to deal with the camels! While living in Afghanistan I learned of a curse the Afghans would speak against their enemies: 'May the fleas of a thousand camel drivers curse you and your family for ever.' Camels are dirty: they spit, they bite, they urinate on you if you turn your back on them, and they

---

[7] 2 Corinthians 1:9

[8] 2 Corinthians 1:9, *The Message*

[9] 2 Corinthians 6:1–2, *The Message*

have fleas. Only one thing is dirtier than a camel, and that is a camel driver!

There is grace from God to respond to the camels, and the camel drivers! After a recent time of testing, I came to the conclusion that God was using the choices of people around me to influence some important decisions in my life. I had no doubt about God's goodness. My temptation was to submit to God, but harbour anger towards the people God was using. I am not saying they made the right choices, but God used their choices to guide me. It was all the more galling to me because they attributed their behaviour to God's leading. As I prayed about my response to these people, I wanted to piously tell God he is greater than people, that I love him, that he works in all things for my good, etc., etc., but I couldn't wait to sit down and tell the people who had offended me what I thought of them. I had mental conversations giving them a piece of my mind. It felt really good! No doubt that is the place to deal with anger: alone with God. But being honest with God does not include taking up an offence or allowing bitterness to take root in our hearts. God offered me grace to accept his leading, and to respond aright in my heart. I had to take hold of his grace and apply it, in order not to be distracted from God's plan and purpose for me.

How do you deal with the camels and the 'camel drivers' in your life? May I suggest the most important words to add to your vocabulary in dealing with the camel drivers is 'no'? Say no to bitterness, so no to busyness, say no to living in too many circles in life, say no to more and bigger and better material possessions, and say no to your kids when it means rushing from one activity to another all week long. Say no to the job offer that will take you away from your *ecclesia*. Say no to withdrawing from your simple church because you are offended by someone in the group or missing all the programmes of big church. And say yes to God. Say yes to his offer of grace to live for his glory. Say yes to God, or you will be captured by the camels and carried away captive.

There are 'seven camels' I want to point out that I have faced in my life, or seen others face. Let me describe them to you so you can identify the 'camels' that have distracted you from a focused obedience to the purposes of God. I have a suggestion before I go further. Instead of reading further, taking in what I share as interesting or helpful information, why not stop right now and ask God to alert you if you are in danger of running into a camel? Maybe you feel like you are the one lying in the road, run over by the camel!? Maybe it's not the camels that bother you, but the camel drivers? Regardless, I encourage you to set this book aside and ask God to prepare your heart to hear anything that could keep you from living a life of fierce faithfulness to him and his purposes lived through you.

Seven camels that distract us

Camel # 1 – Dabbling

Are you a spiritual dabbler? Do you borrow from other people's walks with God, but have little or no intimacy with the Father yourself? Are you constantly shifting focus in your life, running after the newest, latest 'prevailing word of the Lord' as some people call it? Is it hard for you to put down roots emotionally in a community of people and build deep friendships of trust and accountability? If your answer to these questions is yes, you may have developed a pattern in your life of spiritual dabbling. To dabble literally means to have a casual or superficial interest in something, to paddle, play or splash in the water. Spiritual dabbling may feel good, but God has much more for you.

To dabble literally means ... to paddle, play, or splash in the water. Spiritual dabbling may feel good, but God has much more for you.

A big conference here, a little book there, a new CD, the latest revelation in a prophetic Internet newsletter . . . all these can be forms of dabbling. Why is it that we run from one source of life to another when God himself wants to be everything we need? Sure, there is a place to learn from others. But is he your main source? Is he your inspiration, comfort, guidance, significance and security? Human resources won't carry you through personal testing from God, nor do they have what it takes to enable you to discern the distractions the enemy puts on your pathway.

All of us, especially leaders and Christian workers, have a tendency to get our spiritual food from others rather than spending consistent, extended time alone with God daily. The psalmist David said he called upon the Lord every day:

I call daily upon You. . .[10]

Dabblers cannot and will not be able to speak life to dry bones; they are too distracted by too many 'good' things. Spiritual dabblers do not have what it takes to hear God's voice and live a life of radical obedience. Maybe you did at one time, but is your obedience current? Is your faith growing and focused? Are you taking on new challenges to believe God for more people to know him, for him to be glorified in and through your life in greater ways? Do you weep over your friends to be saved? Do you fast for family members who don't know Jesus? Do you intercede for those you lead? When was the last time you got alone in your bedroom, shut your door, and lay on the floor before God and wept out of hunger and desire to be in his presence? In the name of being balanced and faithful, have you backed away from going hard after God and his purposes for your life? Have you reacted to religious extremists and allowed cynicism to creep into your way of seeing things?

If you are a spiritual dabbler, repent now. Cry out to God for

---

[10] Psalm 88:9

passion, real sacrificial, radical, going-all-out for Jesus passion. If you seek him like you are searching for a lost treasure, if you lift up your voice and cry out to him, if you become desperate again for God, he will hear you and he will answer.[11] He will breathe life on the valley of death where dry bones lay lifeless in your heart.

Camel # 2 – Plateauing

We plateau when we stop growing. A plateau is a period or phase when there is little increase in our life. It is a season of life intended for our personal growth and development in which little headway is being made. God invites us to a lifetime of learning and spiritual growth. He is continually at work in us to form us to be like his son, Jesus.

It says in Psalm 103 that God showed the children of Israel his mighty acts, but he taught Moses his ways. God enjoys teaching us his ways. He invites us to partner with him. He longs for friendship with us. Some people keep growing all their lives. We refer to them as 'lifetime learners'. It's because they know the ways of God. Others reach a stage where they stop growing because they are not learning spiritually. They become spiritually stagnant, they dry up on the inside. To change the metaphor from the plateau: their heart is like a valley of dry bones.

Spiritual growth cannot be separated from the testings of God. God tests those he loves.[12] If we, or others around us, don't create the circumstances that test us, you can be sure that God will do it for us. He loves us too much to leave us on our own. If we fail the tests God takes us through, we plateau.

I have nothing against big churches, but they can be convenient places of hiding for those who have plateaued spiritually, including the pastor or others on the staff of the church. You can

---

[11] Proverbs 2:3–5

[12] Genesis 22:1; Deuteronomy 8:2; Psalm 11:4-5; 105:19; Jeremiah 17:10

'go to church' and hide in the church. If this is you, you need to take time to do some serious spiritual homework if you are going to get off the plateau and move on to higher ground.

> *If we fail the tests God takes us through, we plateau.*

One of the reasons there are so many biographies in the Bible is to illustrate how God tests and trains those who follow him, especially those who lead others. He tested David by calling him to be a king and then allowing him to be under Saul for many years. He tested Moses by giving him a people to lead that were stubborn and unteachable. He tested Abraham when he asked him to offer up his son as a sacrifice. He tested Joseph by giving him a dream that he would rule over his brothers and then allowed his brothers to reject and betray him. He tested Daniel, and Paul and John Mark. We are all tested and taught by God. Not just the great heroes in the Bible, but every one of us.

If you have reached a spiritual plateau, it may be because you have failed to pass or even discern a test God was taking you through. When Moses struck a rock in the wilderness, he failed a test. When David sent his troops into battle, and stayed home and lusted after his neighbour's wife, he failed a test. When Joseph prematurely declared the dream God gave him that he would rule over his brothers, he failed a test. Thankfully, failed tests are not final to God. There are no 'failures' to God if we humble ourselves and ask for mercy. God sees us through eyes of faith: how he intends to bring us out on the other side of the test.

What do we do if we are stuck on a plateau? We ask God to give us a new beginning. We cry out to God, we lift our voice to him and cry out for his forgiveness. We humble ourselves before God *and people*. We receive by faith the grace to go through our test – God offers us enabling grace for every test and trial and temptation we face. We ask God to help us discern why we have plateaued if we don't know the reason already. We commit our-selves to obey God no matter what the cost. Unconditional obe-dience is what God is after. Nothing else will do. We spend time daily worshipping God and reading his word. We ask God for a new beginning, and step out in faith when he gives it to us. We risk everything to start climbing again.

If you are serious about changing the way you do church, it will take courage to acknowledge you are on a plateau and need to climb higher. You are going to have to exercise some spiritual muscles that may not have been used in a long time. Better to do it now before they atrophy completely.

Perhaps it is how you do church that is one of the distractions in your life? If so, it is time for some serious assessment.

> *God takes everyone through the valley of dry bones to teach us we don't have what it takes in ourselves to serve in God's army.*

God takes everyone through the valley of dry bones to teach us we don't have what it takes in ourselves to serve in God's army. Passion is refined in seasons of testing. Passion is about suffering, and the deepest and purest passion for God is purified in the fires of great affliction. Some of the most passionate people I know have faced seasons of depression, horrible anxiety attacks, deep feelings of abandonment by God, severe physical affliction, and rejection from people. Yet they have come out on the other side more passionate for God. They climbed off the plateau they were on though it felt like they had to rock-climb up a mountain wall. It is these people that are the most focused. They have paid the greatest price to regain their focus and their passion. They grew to that place through a desperate determination to get their pas-sion back.

If you have reached a plateau in your relationship with God, remember it is not just about you. God tests us so we will glorify him. He is the source and the goal of our lives, and it is from him and for him that we are empowered to go beyond the plateau to a place where we receive more mercy and he receives greater glory.

Camel # 3 – Inner vows

An inner vow is a promise we make to ourselves, normally in response to pain or difficulty we experience in human relationships. Typically the vows we make use language like, 'I'll never do that again. . .' or 'I won't ever let anyone get that close to me again.' Or, 'Whatever it takes, I will make sure that never happens again.'

We all make such vows. It is human nature to avoid pain. Characteristic of the vows we make are decisions to avoid difficulty or gain approval. Later we'll look at a vow made to the Lord; but this kind of vow is normally about self-protection, punishing others, getting even, proving something to someone, or doing something to feel comforted or accepted by others.

The problem with making vows is that they imprison our heart. They set us on a course of action that locks us into a certain kind of behaviour. Vows determine how we think and how we see. An ungodly inner vow gets us locked into idolatrous thinking patterns that become an inner belief system. Vows become values, but not good values. Inner vows shape our decisions, determine the level of risks we will take, infect our thinking about ourselves and about God. Inner vows deceive our spirits.

Ungodly inner vows rob us of true passion.

Ungodly inner vows rob us of true passion. Because they are based on fear, shame, unbelief and a drive to prove ourselves to others, they rob us of our freedom to obey God. Or we strive to obey God for the wrong reasons. Inner vows can be discerned through the help of the Holy Spirit or a good counsellor,[13] and they can be broken through the power of the cross.[14]

Camel # 4 – Unclear vision

Nothing is more confusing to people than a leader or a person who frequently changes direction. I call this 'blowing an unsteady trumpet'. When the sound of a trumpet warbles or is off key, it does not inspire anyone, and it certainly doesn't make great music.

A form of trumpet, called a bugle, was used in the days of the cavalry in the American West to communicate to the troops in time of battle. It was used to signal the men to 'regroup and charge the enemy lines'. The bugle was also used to signal retreat, or a call to parade, or let the troops know it was 'chow time'. If the commanding officer had had one tune after another blown in the time of battle, it would have confused and demoralized the troops. They would have lost confidence in their commanding officer.

The same is true for spiritual leaders. Vision can be intoxicating. Sadly, spiritual vision can also be an end in itself. There is a kind of exhilaration, a form of adrenalin rush, that comes from hearing a new idea and getting excited about it. So much so that some leaders live for the rush they get from casting a new vision and getting everyone hyped up about it. New vision can be a camel in the road to keep us from being faithful to the last thing

---

[13] I recommend a one-week retreat called 'Healing for the Nations' led by Steve and Rujon Morrison. HFTN is the most powerful one-week retreat I have come across. You can get more information about the retreat at their website, www.healingforthe-nations.org. I have recommended HFTN to leaders from all over the world and all of them have testified to its great value for their lives.

[14] For more on inner vows and how to break them, I recommend Robert McGee's book, *The Search for Significance*, Thomas Nelson 2003.

God called us to do. If God has spoken, then blow the trumpet and call the people to action. But don't call them to action in one direction, and then blow it again and ask them to charge in another direction. If you are seeking direction, find out what God is saying, and stick with it. Don't change because it gets tough, or because it is more exciting to move on to something new.

> *Faithfulness is a long journey of obedience in the same direction, empowered by the sweet-tasting grace of God.*

Godly passion grows as a response to a clear, steady, consistent vision of God's glory saturating the planet through movements of organic and obedient churches. Know what part God has given you in this worldwide movement of movements and stick with it. Don't waver and don't look for new direction when things get tough. Stick with what God says. It may take many years of consistent obedience to realize all God has planned to bring about through your life. Faithfulness is a long journey of obedience in the same direction, empowered by the sweet-tasting grace of God.

Camel # 5 – Financial security

There is nothing wrong with investing or planning for the future. But Western culture is obsessed with accumulating wealth and guaranteeing future security. This obsession is excessive and passion robbing. Financial planners do a fine service for those who need help in planning for the future, but they don't speak for God. The most God-glorifying gathering I have attended on the subject of finances was called 'Generous Giving'. The name says it all. Good stewardship is not about accumulating but giving, not about hoarding but sharing. God expects us to be wise stewards, and that includes investing and making a profit. But the treasures that will be enjoyed for ever are those that are the result of investing in people's lives for eternity, not the ones stored up on Wall Street.

> *The treasures that will be enjoyed for ever are those that are the result of investing in people's lives for eternity, not the ones stored up on Wall Street.*

One slight tug by the hand of God and the rug could be pulled out from under the global economy. Everything we have saved could vanish overnight. So don't put your trust in riches. Don't look for security from man or the financial systems of man. Don't believe the hype. If you feel led by God to invest in pensions and savings plans, go ahead. But invest primarily in spreading the gospel. The only thing you can take to heaven besides your own heart is the people you influence for God. That is the fruit that remains.

If you experience a loss of fervour for spreading the gospel, it may be in direct proportion to the amount of time you are occupied with your future security. If that is the case, it's time for some honest evaluation. Jesus said it very clearly:

> Do not lay up for yourselves treasures on earth, where moth and rust destroy and where thieves break in and steal; but lay up for yourselves treasures in heaven . . . for where your treasure is, there your heart will be also. . .[15]

Camel # 6 – Frantic pace of life

Who says we have to own a 'nice' home? Or drive a new car? Or that our kids have to be involved in four sports a year? I know some parents who keep a spreadsheet on their computer to keep

---

[15] Matthew 6:19–21

up with the activities of their kids. Don't buy into the lie that the world determines how fast a pace of life you must live. And don't let your kids buy into it either.

If there are no margins in your life, you will not have time to hear God. If there is no space, no free time for you to read and reflect, how can you be refuelled emotionally and spiritually? Passion for Jesus and his purposes in life are chosen, then nurtured by those who refuse to let the world shape them in it's mould. You are free to say no. If you don't, the camel of frantic living will hunt you down, run you over and then dance on your grave!

> *The camel of frantic living will hunt you down, run you over and then dance on your grave!*

Camel # 7 – Conventional churchianity

Conventional ways of doing church in many instances have become a camel in the road to distract us from real church. In his book, *The Present Future*, Reggie McNeal voices what many people have known in their heart but lacked the words to say. He says, '. . .the church culture in North America is on life support. It is living off the work, money, and energy of previous generations. . .' The same can be said for church in Australia, South Africa and the UK. McNeal believes the culture we call church is either dead or about to die: 'This culture has become confused with biblical Christianity, both inside the church and out.'[16] Postmodern youth do not want church as a machine and they don't want leaders who serve as mechanics to keep the machine running. They are searching for something far more meaningful in

---

[16] Reggie McNeal, *The Present Future: Six Tough Questions for the Church*, Jossey-Bass (Wiley) 2003, p 1.

their experience of church. They are willing to toss out institutional church to find it, and rightfully so.

> *Many people are leaving institutional churches, not because they don't believe in church, but because they do believe in it.*

Erwin McManus speaks the truth when he says God is not unwilling to stand against the very church he started:

> Two thousand years ago God started a revolt against the religion he started. So don't ever put it past God to cause a groundswell against churches and Christian institutions that bear His name. If he was willing to turn Judaism upside down, don't think for a moment our institutions are safe from a divine revolt. I am convinced that even now there are multitudes of followers of Jesus Christ who are sick and tired of the church playing games and playing down the call of God. My travels only confirm that the murmurings of revolution are everywhere. I am convinced that there is an uprising in the works and that no one less than God is behind it.[17]

Many people are leaving institutional churches, not because they don't believe in church, but because they do believe in it. They are not leaving because they have lost their faith, they are leaving so they won't lose their faith. The church has become a hindrance to the spiritual growth of many people. David Barrett and Todd Johnson estimate there are 112 million 'churchless Christians' worldwide. They project that the number will double in the next 20 years.[18] George Barna estimates that 53,000 people a week are leaving the church in America. The same pattern has been true for many years in Britain and Australia, and started happening after 1994 in South Africa.

Why have so many left the church? They haven't! You can

---

[17] Erwin McManus, *The Barbarian Way*, Thomas Nelson 2005, p 114.

[18] Reggie McNeal, *The Present Future: Six Tough Questions for the Church*, p 4.

never be any less church than you already are as a follower of Jesus. What many people have discovered, and many institutional church leaders have yet to realize, is that church is who you are, not where you go. Church in its essence is gathering with two or three others who love and obey Jesus, but it doesn't have to be two or three thousand. Sadly, many people are so addicted to the programmes of the church, they aren't able to enjoy the beauty of simple, organic church. Institutional church has made them weak instead of strong. They need others to do church for them.

Those who are leaders in institutional church can easily become impressed with their own importance. They can sway crowds with powerful words. Their vision can move people to make great sacrifices. If institutional church leaders are not careful, in the name of church they will hinder people from experiencing church as God intended it. They can easily become infatuated with their own programmes and passions. Sadly, God's glory can be replaced in their hearts by ideas of their own importance.

> *If leaders are not careful, in the name of church they will hinder people from experiencing church as God intended it.*

The church doesn't need leaders; it needs humble leaders. God gave leaders to the church to spread his glory, not to be seen as glorious in the eyes of people. The church doesn't need leaders who speak against new ways of doing church or defend the old ways. God is a God of order, but that doesn't mean he won't move against the order of man and create some holy disorder to get people to experience church as he intended it. Anyone who thinks Jesus came to be a defender of the status quo is reading a different Bible from the one I read. It takes some serious revising of Scripture to picture a Jesus who was the advocate of orderly tradition. With his small band of followers he started a revolution. He instituted an uprising that led eventually to a worldwide movement that spread to all nations. The uprising Jesus started was not begun to defend the positions of the powerful, but to up-end the religious institutions of the day and bring people into a missional movement that transcends culture, tribe, race, age and gender.

Leaders in the church are messengers. It is the glory of the message we carry, not the powerful personality of the messenger, that is to inspire the church. The message we carry is about a church for every man and woman, boy and girl. It is about a God of the people, all the people. When we reach the end of the age, and we join the redeemed from every tribe and nation and fall on our faces to worship the Lamb who is worthy, who will notice that church as we know it is no more? Leadership positions and titles are temporary at best, but the Lamb is for ever.

Many great leaders who have gone before us never lived to see the promises God gave them fulfilled. Hebrews 11 describes a parade of men and women of faith who heard from God, stepped out in faith to obey him, and did not see with their own eyes the fulfilment of the dream God put in their heart. They were humble enough not to create something out of impatience, and then call it faith. They waited for God to act.

The writer to the Hebrews says about them:

> . . .they all died in faith, not having received the promises, but having seen them afar off. . .[19]

We measure greatness by how big an institutional church becomes, how many books an author has written, or how moving a person is as a speaker. But God measures greatness by how faithful we are to him.

One focus above all others

The one thing that transcends all others, the focus we are to have above everything else, is the glory of God. That's all that matters.

---

[19] Hebrews 11:13

If we are focused on his glory, and we have a right understanding of what his glory is, then we will not strive in the flesh to defend church structures that are more of a hindrance to God's glory than a help. Church as we know it may have to die to discover what church for our culture is truly about. Jesus spoke about new wineskins. Wineskins were made from the skin of sacrificed animals. New wineskins require sacrifice. Blood has to be shed. It is not a small thing to make room for new wineskins.[20]

The glory of God is ultimate, not the spiritual gifts God gave us to spread his glory. When this age is over, and we bow in his presence, followers of Jesus will long for one thing, and that is to look into his eyes and see the pleasure and joy he receives when we lay our treasures, our crowns, at his feet. That's what we strive to see: the delight Jesus has when we bring him more worship through laying crowns before him.

Our ultimate goal is not how impressive our prayers are, or how many poor we feed, or the leaders we train, or the churches we plant, or great programmes we start, or any of the things we do for him. This is *the* dream, the one thing that counts at the end of time, to be able to look into those beautiful, piercing eyes and know that he is worshipped and enjoyed and loved by those we have brought to him. That is our reward. That is enough. We ask no more than that. This is what energizes and focuses everything we do in his name.

I love the church, but church is not the goal of what we do. Jesus is the goal. I am not very good at church, and to be really honest, I don't know many people who are. But that's okay, because it's not about us.

> The ultimate reward of every true Jesus-follower is not what rewards he or she receives on earth, but the reward the Lamb receives in heaven.

---

[20] Matthew 9:17

You have a choice about this dear friend: at the end of time you can stand before God with empty hands, or you can come to him with crowns to lay before him. The ultimate reward of every true Jesus-follower is not what rewards he or she receives on earth, but the reward the Lamb receives in heaven. Paul said,

> For what is our hope, or joy, or crown of rejoicing? Is it not even you in the presence of our Lord Jesus Christ. . .?[21]

The glory God receives through the worship of those who love him is both the fuel and the goal of all we do. It's the fuel because it is what empowers us to press on. It is the goal because the work of leading and pioneering and serving has but one ultimate goal, and that is the pleasure and joy of bringing the poor and the lost into the experience of his mercy and goodness. The enjoyment of the Lamb for ever is the only thing that lasts for ever. Everything else is secondary. John wrote at the end of his life:

> Thou art worthy, O Lord, to receive glory and honour and power: for thou hast created all things, and for thy pleasure they are created.[22]

Sold out Jesus-followers will never cry from the depths of their being, 'Worthy is the Lamb', who have not seen him and savoured him. To quote John Piper:

> If the pursuit of God's glory is not ordered above the pursuit of man's good in the affections of the heart and the priorities of the church, man will not be well served and God will not be duly honored. . .[23]

It quite often happens that we are distracted from the God we serve by the work we do for God. In fact, if we're not careful, the work we do for God can end up being a big ugly, biting, spitting, flea-ridden camel! When Moses was at the end of himself as a leader, he cried out, 'Show me your glory!'[24] If your passion has dried up, there is only one place to go to get it back, and that is

---

[21] 1 Thessalonians 2:19   [22] Revelation 4:11

[23] John Piper, *Let the Nations Be Glad*.   [24] Exodus 33:18

to get alone with God. Even now, you may want to get on your knees and cry out to God. Ask him for a fresh revelation of his glory.

Three questions about God's glory

What is the glory of God?

It's hard, if not impossible, to live for what we cannot see and do not understand. For years all I knew of the glory of God was what I heard in church: it was an expression of exuberant praise by worshippers in the little Pentecostal churches my father pastored. Growing up in an atmosphere of emotionally charged worship had its good and bad sides. The good was to see the sincerity of the people who loved Jesus and had turned from alcohol and bar-room brawls to follow him. The bad included a lack of depth and content to the worship. 'Glory to God!' was a common expression for the happy believers who jumped and shouted and praised the Lord in the churches my father pastored. But what did it really mean to give glory to God? As I grew older I noticed that the exclamations of praise by the believers seemed to pick up in volume in proportion to a lack of authenticity and consistency in their lives. 'Glory!' became a sort of Christian slang expression, exclaimed with a certain warble in the voice as well and a slight shake of the head. I became sceptical of the folks who had one voice for God and another voice for the rest of us.

'Glory!' became a sort of Christian slang expression

My puzzlement grew over the years as I read statements about God's glory in the Bible. I still love the sound of the expression, 'the glory of the Lord'. It holds a certain mystery and wonder to me, but I didn't have a clue what it meant for many years. I did

some word studies, and compared verses, but there was little revelation about this most mysterious, but awesomely meaningful of
terms. One day, as I read the following words written by the
prophet Habakkuk, I knew I had to learn more. I was stirred about
God's promise given to Habakkuk. I could not give up until I knew
what God meant when he spoke through the prophet:

> . . .the earth will be filled with the knowledge of the glory of the
> LORD, as the waters cover the sea.[25]

Something stirs deep in my spirit when I read those words: if God
is going to cover the earth with his glory, I want to be part of it.
But what is it that I want to be part of? It's his plan to reveal his
glory globally, but what exactly does that mean? How will he do
it? I know people who believe the glory of the Lord is feeling
God's presence. But surely there is more than feeling God's presence to 'the glory of the Lord'? In my search for answers to these
questions, I read about Paul's fierce passion to preach so the
'glory of God's mercy' would be extended to those who did not
know God. Paul wrote:

> . . .so the Gentiles might glorify God for his mercy . . . I have made it
> my aim to preach the gospel, not where Christ was already named.[26]

As I gave myself to serious contemplation about the centrality of
God's glory in Paul's writing and thinking, I became convinced
that this revelation shaped Paul's understanding of the church. If
we are to change the way we do church, we must first change
the reason we do church. Paul understood by revelation from the
Holy Spirit that the church was the channel through which God
was going to fill the earth with his glory. And it was this revelation that determined everything about Paul's life. Should it not
have the same effect on ours as well? The Spirit taught Paul that
the ache in every human heart is for Jesus, the face of God to this
world. He knew as well that we've all been blinded by the god of

---

[25] Habakkuk 2:14, NIV   [26] Romans 15:9, 20, NIV

this age. John Piper captures the heart of Paul's insight in these moving words:

> No one goes to the Grand Canyon to increase self-esteem. Why do we go? Because there is greater healing for the soul in beholding splendor than there is in beholding self. Indeed, what could be more ludicrous in a vast and glorious universe like this than a human being, on the speck called earth, standing in front of a mirror trying to find significance in his own self-image? It is a great sadness that this is the gospel of the modern world.[27]

God's glory is to be the focus of our life together as the family of God. This is the core, the nexus, the centre of our corporate being. The glory of God is the sparking, fixed point of a chaotic world. As the Westminster Confession states, 'The chief end of man is to glorify God and enjoy him for ever.' It was a revelation of the glory of God in Christ Jesus that transformed Paul on the road to Damascus – it is that same glory that will keep on transforming us. If his glory is not our main focus, the camels have done their work on us. It is a fresh revelation of his glory that will renew our passion, not better leaders or a great model of church, not money, fame or security. Nothing else.

Not only was God's glory the focus of Paul's life, it is the focus of God himself. He is devoted to his own glory. It was God who inspired Isaiah to write these words:

> For my own sake, for my own sake, I will do it . . . I will not give my glory to another. . .[28]

No place in Scripture has helped me see and grasp and enjoy the glory of God more than Moses' encounter with God in Exodus 33 and 34. I cannot describe the delight and relief I experienced when I discovered God's glory in these chapters. It almost seemed I was there with Moses as God revealed to him his glory.

---

[27] John Piper, *Seeing and Savouring Jesus Christ*, IVP 2005 (UK) and Crossway 2004 (US). [28] Isaiah 48:11

When Moses asked God to show him his glory, God told him he could not see it and live. God's glory would kill him. But God saw the desire and desperation of Moses, so he placed him in the cleft of a rock, turned his back towards him, and God passed by. He revealed only a small portion of himself, but what Moses saw was the wonder of God's own being, his goodness, his kindness, his mercy and compassion:

> And Moses said, "Please, show me Your glory." Then God said, "I will make all My *goodness* pass before you . . . I will be *gracious* to whom I will be gracious, and I will have *compassion* on whom I will have compassion . . . And the Lord passed before him and proclaimed, "The Lord, the Lord God, *merciful* and *gracious*, *longsuffering*, and *abounding in goodness and truth*, *keeping mercy* for thousands, *forgiving iniquity* and transgression and sin." [29]

God's glory is who he is; more than his creation, more than his mighty acts and miracles, more than sensing his presence with us, it is God's awesome, amazing, majestic, blinding beauty. The Hebrew word for 'glory' literally means weight or substance. The opposite of glory is lightweight, superficial or empty. God is heavy, real, the substance of all that is good and true. In other words, church for the sake of church is lightweight, but church for God's glory is the real thing. Everything else is empty and superficial.

Let those words soak into your soul. I pray that, if your passion has died out, or been based on fleshly ambitions, or borrowed from others, or you have no idea what it really is, you would ask God to show himself to you as he did to Moses. I pray that you will pledge yourself to live for this one thing: that the knowledge of the glory of the Lord will fill the whole earth.

---

[29] Exodus 33:18 – 34:7

I pray that, if your passion has died out, or been based on fleshly ambitions, or borrowed from others, or you have no idea what it really is, you would ask God to show himself to you as he did to Moses.

Where is the glory of God?

But wait, there is more. Jesus said, 'The glory you have given to me, I have given to them.'[30] God's glory is about God, but it's *given to us*? Jesus gave the glory of God to his followers. How can this be? How is it that the glory that would have killed Moses if he saw it was given to ordinary disciples, to fishermen, tax collectors, and terrorists?[31] Indeed, this is part of the unfolding mystery that so captured the soul of the great apostle Paul. He received the revelation that God has chosen to make us, the church collective, a living temple. We are the dwelling place of his glory on earth. Just as the glory of God filled Solomon's Temple when he dedicated it to the Lord, so God's glory dwells in us, the church, when we dedicate our lives to God. That is why Paul wrote:

> . . .you are being built into a dwelling place of God on earth . . . to God be glory in the church . . . to all generations![32]

No wonder God took back his church from a few religious leaders and gave it to his people. Some time ago, God spoke to my friend John Scholtz, lead pastor of Harvest Church in Port Elizabeth, South Africa, and told him, 'Give my church back to my people.' The church was designed by God to be simple, accessible,

---

[30] John 17:22

[31] Simon the Zealot was a member of a group called the Zealots, who were committed to the violent overthrow of the Roman occupying force.

[32] Ephesians 2:22; 3:21

available to everyone. No wonder he gave a few leaders to equip the whole church for ministry. He wanted all his people involved. He wanted every single person called, gifted and strategically placed where they could serve him to maximum effectiveness. He did not choose an elite few to reveal his glory, but all his people. His intention is to use ordinary people to show off his extraordinary greatness to the whole earth.

This mystery that I began to understand many years ago, has struck me again and again. God is going to saturate the planet with himself – through the church. He is going to do it through you and me and others like us. Not through meetings and programmes and schools and conferences, but through people. Through *his* people. Through the living, loving and sometimes sinning people of God, he will make his glory known, one person, one family, one village, one business, one school, one tribe and nation at a time.

> **God is going to saturate the planet with himself - through the church.**

How will God fill the earth with his glory? The same way Jesus made the glory of his Father seen and known when he came to earth. Jesus worked, ate and stayed with people in their homes. He took care of his mother, went to weddings, attended religious ceremonies and hung out with ordinary people. Filling the earth with the glory of the Lord means filling every Tesco's, Mugg & Bean and Starbucks with a band of Jesus' followers. It means getting into every mall and village, every campus and business, and penetrating every neighbourhood and nation with a Jesus community. Filling the earth with the glory of God means filling it with simple-church communities of Jesus-followers that hang out with people the same way Jesus hung out with people.

After hearing me speak about the glory of God and God's desire to fill the earth with his glory, one young person said to me,

'You're just trying to convince me to be a missionary.' I was talking about what God desires to do in the earth, she heard she had to go as a missionary. I responded by saying something like, 'Going to other nations is a wonderful calling of course, but what I'm speaking about is much more encompassing than being a missionary. I am not trying to get anyone to go anywhere, but I am fiercely committed to influencing all those I can to live their lives for one passion above all others, that is God's glory. It's first of all about who and what we live for, not where we go.'

The problem with this young lady was that she was focused on geography, thinking that to live supremely for God's glory was to go to Mongolia or some other place on the planet she didn't want to go. Of course we can't live for his glory if we refuse to go to Mongolia. But the issue is not where we go for God, but when we see his glory *do we want to go somewhere for him*?

This is the difference between missions and mission. I have dropped the word 'missions' from my vocabulary. Most people think that to be a missionary you have to be called, which means those who aren't missionaries are not called. If you are not called, you are a spiritual wuss, or you wouldn't be hanging out at the local pub like you do. But when you drop the 's' from missions, you have mission. There is one mission, and it's God's mission. God's mission is God's glory. He has chosen to reveal his glory through the church. Everyone who is part of God's church is called to spread God's glory. Our mission is the same as God's: his glory in the earth. The question is not 'Are you called?' but 'Where are you called?'

This is why there is so much confusion about knowing God's will. Too many people try to discover God's will for their lives by asking the wrong questions: What should I do? Where do I go? When do I do it? Those questions have their place, but the most important question must precede them, and that is: 'God, will you show me your glory?' Finding God's will flows naturally from seeing, savouring and surrendering our lives to his glory. When we see his glory, receiving instructions about where he wants us to go is a small matter indeed.

When we are wholly devoted to Jesus, we naturally make ourselves available to make Jesus known to others. When we are passionate for Jesus, we will be passionate for those he is passionate about. Surrender to God follows seeing God. It was natural for Isaiah to say 'send me' because he had seen the Lord. It is a lack of seeing that causes a lack of going.

> **Seeking to know the will of God without a revelation of the glory of God will lead to resisting, reacting and negotiating over the will of God.**

Seeking to know the will of God without a revelation of the glory of God will lead to resisting, reacting and negotiating over the will of God. As long as we are resistant to going certain places for God, we are obviously not impressed with God himself. We are still serving a God of our own making. But when we see him in his awesome splendour, we will not negotiate with him about his will for our lives. When we see him, then surrender to him, only then is it time to ask the detailed questions of where and when to serve him. Not to see him is to make surrender to him all the more difficult. But when we see him, no place or people will scare us or impress us – we will be far more impressed with God.

How will God fill the earth with his glory? He will fill the earth with glory by filling it with his church, with communities of people who love him and make him known to others. He told Adam and Eve to be fruitful and multiply and fill the earth.[33] This command goes back to God's original intention for creating us in the first place. He wants a people that is made up of every people on the earth. He wants a people who will share his delight in showing

---

[33] Genesis 1:28

mercy to those who don't know him. He has always wanted to fill the earth with his goodness by filling it with those who know and love him.

Why the glory of God?

God will fill the earth with his goodness and kindness and beauty to fill it with the worship of his Son. The mission of God is the worship of his Son by all the peoples of the earth. It's so people from every tribe and tongue and nation and people will worship the Lamb. I believe the most intense longings of the human heart and the deepest meaning of heaven and earth are summed up in this phrase: the glory of God. The church was created to show it, and we were made to see it and savour it. Nothing less will do.[34]

This is the vision, the focus, the main thing we live our lives for. Don't let the camels on the road distract or sideline you. Press into God. Seek him to see him and to savour him. Do this and then you will know that God and God alone will restore passion to your soul and empower you to impart life to the dry bones of his church. Those who have seen God's glory are filled with passion. It is this passion that I call apostolic passion. Without it we can have a big car but only a little engine: lots of steel but no power to get where we're going.

---

[34] John Piper, *Seeing and Savouring Jesus Christ*, p 19.

PART FOUR
Apostolic Passion

6

Big Cars with Very Little Engines

Imagine a well-dressed businessman who walks out the front door of his big mansion of a house, strolls down the path, and once again climbs in his shiny big car, ready for work. He closes the driver's door with a smile, when he hears the heavy thunk of a very well made, tightly engineered automobile. As he grips the steering wheel with both hands, he notices one of his neighbours pulling out of the drive, heading for work as well. He offers a friendly salute to his fellow commuter, and turns his eyes back towards the road.

The day drags on as Mr Businessman waves and grins at those who walk or drive by. His big-boy car draws appreciative glances, and he waves at them all. After a full day of sitting in his car, pointed in the direction of work, he piles out, stretches, and heads back to the house.

What's wrong in this picture? He never goes to work. He sits all day in the driver's seat, hands on the wheel, cheerily waving at passers-by, and goes nowhere. The car is pointed in the right direction, the businessman is decked out and ready for work, but the car never moves. Why? Because there is a great big car, but a tiny little sewing-machine motor where a V6 engine belongs.

Stunning vision and mission statements will get a church no

further than the poster paper on which they are written, if they are not empowered by a lived-out set of apostolic core values.

It takes apostolic passion to lift an apostolic vision. By apostolic passion I mean a set of core values that empower us to live radically as the early apostles lived. They delegated money matters and pastoral concerns so they could devote themselves to caring for the poor and preaching to the lost. They were bold, focused, and committed to radical obedience, no matter what it cost them. They were zealous to see people meet Jesus. They were ridiculed, persecuted and beaten for their faith. Perhaps the reason some modern-day 'apostles' don't suffer a similar fate is that they don't live a similar lifestyle.

The church is in trouble. To illustrate how deeply we are in trouble, a sobering look at the facts in the United States might be helpful. Although it's not the same in every country, the trend is mirrored in many other places. Consider these realities:

○ The largest Protestant denomination in the United States is the Southern Baptists. They have reported that only 4 per cent of their churches will plant a daughter church.
○ Recent research about church attendance across all denominations in America has shown that, although the population of the United States grew by 13.2 per cent from 1900 to 2000, church attendance grew by just 3 per cent during that same time frame. From 2000 to 2004 the United States population grew by 4 per cent while the church grew only 0.8 % during the same time period.
○ Jesus-believing churches in the US have failed to add even 2 per cent of the American population to the church in the last 50 years.
○ One of the most staggering facts to be discovered through recent research is that over 4,000 churches close their doors every year in America, while an average of 1,350 new churches are started annually. Another statistic makes the picture starkly

clear: only 4 per cent of those born between 1977 and 1994 in the US are Christians. This is the most unchurched generation ever in America.[1]

o By the year 2020, at the current rate, only 14 per cent of Americans will attend church, and by 2050, church attendance in the USA could be less than 10 per cent.[2]

Part of the problem is that we don't know we're in trouble. We are losing ground while millions around us are dying without Christ. We need men and women with apostolic passion. Western Christianity is dying and we are happily waving at the world as it dies.

Islam may be God's gift to stir the church out of its slumber

While the passion of so much of the Western church turns further and further from suffering and sacrifice, Islam is mounting a worldwide challenge to win Western nations to their faith. Caring deeply for the church in the West, and at the same time believing what will save the church is embracing a vision far bigger than singing Christmas carols in a mall once a year, I felt led several years ago to invite a group of friends to join me on an unusual journey into the heart of the Sinai Desert.

We must have seemed like a very strange group to our Egyptian bus driver. He had driven us deep into the Sinai Desert, close to the Red Sea. We asked him to drive us to the end of the most remote road we could find on the map, and then drop us there. We were surrounded by sun-scorched, blackened mountains, and miles of barren desert. It was a wild, bleak, uncultivated place.

'Come back for us in two hours,' I told the driver as he reluctantly drove away.

---

[1] American Society for Church Growth, 'Enlarging Our Borders', 1999.
[2] Ibid.

'Here we are,' I said, facing the group of 20 men and women. Strange as it may seem, we were in the Sinai to make a covenant with God. We were leaders of a mission organization, assembled to oversee the affairs of the group we served.

> *Strange as it may seem, we were in the Sinai to make a covenant with God.*

'Walk as far in different directions as you feel comfortable, find a rock, and bring it back here in an hour. Please be reflective as you search for a rock to bring back for the altar. Ask God to show you your part of the covenant,' I said. And then we went into the desert in search of stones to build an altar.

The desert land around us was flat and barren except for a few scrawny bushes here and there. Rocks were not easy to find. Sixty minutes later we assembled. Some brought small rocks you could hold in one hand, a few came with football-sized rocks, and three of our group brought with them a mini-boulder, carrying it together.

We piled our rocks in a makeshift altar, and knelt silently in prayer. Each one made a personal commitment, as they felt led in their own hearts. We were quiet as we prayed. We had agreed on building the altar in the desert as a sign of our covenant with God. Later we shared with each other what we vowed to the Lord. Steve and Liz renewed their commitment to share Jesus with Muslims as neighbours, not enemies. Lynn felt deeply stirred to respond to what had taken place in the Crusades against Muslims and Jews 1,000 years earlier. I had an impression to ask followers of Jesus around the world to fast and pray during the month of Ramadan, the month Muslims go without food during daylight hours.

After a time of sharing the passion of our hearts for Muslims, we prayed corporately, making our covenant with God and each other to love Muslims, not hate them; to reach out to them in the name of Jesus; and to believe God for millions of Muslims around the world to discover the beauty of God in the person of Jesus Christ. We reminded each other about the covenant God made with Ishmael, the rejected son of Abraham, almost 3,000 years earlier:

> And as for Ishmael, I have heard his cry. I have blessed him, and will make him fruitful, and will multiply him exceedingly. He shall beget twelve princes, and I will make him a great nation.[3]

The covenant we made with God was in the context of rising tensions in the Middle East. We were deeply aware that one of the greatest challenges facing the church is how to respond to militant Islam. Some Christians believe Israel is God's chosen people and can do no wrong. Their reasoning is that Israel has a divine right to land. Others believe the tensions in the Middle East will not be solved without addressing the wrongs against the Palestinian people, and that despite God's covenant with Israel in the past, they have forfeited their right to land by breaking the covenant they made with God and rejecting the Messiah, Jesus. Whatever one's position is on that difficult subject, we have been given a strange gift in the form of militant Islam. It is an opportunity for the church to rise up, not in a war on terrorism, but in a massive love endeavour, to make disciples for Jesus throughout the Muslim world. We need to match the ardour of suicide bombers with laying down our lives in love, not hate. We must send our children to serve and love and bring good news to Muslims in North Africa, the Middle East, and South and Central Asia.

One of the greatest challenges facing the church is how to respond to militant Islam.

---

[3] Genesis 17:20

In his book, *The Clash of Civilizations*, Harvard professor Samuel Huntington says the twenty-first century will see an increase in global conflicts, especially between major civilizations.[4] He predicts that the battle between the so-called Christian West and the Muslim Middle East will dominate world politics in this century.

Huntington's dark scenario is unfolding before our eyes. In the last decade we have witnessed a sharp rise in tension between Muslims and the 'Christian West'. Radical fundamentalists brought down the Twin Towers in New York, killed hundreds in train and subway bombings in England and Spain, and continue to wreak havoc in Iraq. In response, American and British troops invaded Iraq and Afghanistan, and US Special Forces were sent on missions to the Sudan and Somalia. One American congressman suggested on a radio talk show that we use a nuclear bomb on Mecca and other Islamic holy sites in response to continued Muslim terrorist attacks in the US.[5] With this kind of thinking, and America's continued military presence in the Middle East, Huntington's view of the future is not far away. But there is a better way. God is calling the church to be his, and his heart is reaching out in love to followers of Muhammad.

Muslims are convinced that America is conducting a holy war against them. When President Bush announced the Second Gulf War as a 'crusade', Muslims knew they were right.

What is the answer to the growing tension between the West and Islam? Certainly not more fear, hatred, terrorist attacks, torture of detainees, or ignoring the hundreds of thousands of people in Palestinian refugee camps. There is an answer, but it will be costly to all sides. It's not a political answer but it has political consequences. It's not found in blind allegiance to Israel, nor is it found

---

[4] Samuel Huntington, *The Clash of Civilizations*, Simon & Schuster 1998. Huntington identifies those civilizations as Western, Orthodox, Chinese, Latin American, Islamic, Hindu, Japanese and African.

[5] Rep. Dan Tancredo from Colorado made his inflammatory comments on 14th July 2005 on a Florida talk show.

in Islamic hegemony in the West. I believe the answer is found in the words of Jesus, revered by Muslims and Christians alike. It was his words that inspired the covenant my friends and I made in the Sinai Desert. Jesus calls his church to a radical, passionate love for our enemies, especially those we fear and dislike. He said:

> But I say to you, love your enemies, bless those who curse you, do good to those who hate you, and pray for those who spitefully use you and persecute you. . .[6]

Jesus showed us the answer to hate and violence and fear. His unprejudiced love of Roman soldiers and the terrorists of his day – the Zealots – and his fearless announcement of the rule of God over all nations show us the way out of the clash between cultures and civilizations. Jesus' uncompromising call for the religious conservatives and political liberals of his day to repent and believe his message is our example for how to respond to militant Muslims. Some may see this as another form of fundamentalism, but don't be fooled by their arrogance. Jesus didn't take sides with any political party. He didn't need to. He called all the parties to himself and to the kingdom he proclaimed.

> *Jesus' uncompromising call for the religious conservatives and political liberals of his day to repent and believe his message is our example for how to respond to militant Muslims.*

He asked people on all points of the political spectrum to repent, take up their own cross, and follow him. We must do no less than Jesus. Taking sides with Israelis or Palestinians is not the answer. We must take God's side.

---

[6] Matthew 5:44

What made the wall fall?

When I watched my television screen as the Berlin Wall fell in 1989, something strange stirred in my heart. It was an extraordinary moment in history. What political pundits said would take decades to evolve happened in hours and days. Whole nations threw off the burdensome yoke of Communism overnight. Not just one, or two, but six, eight, even ten nations were transformed in a moment.

As I viewed history in the making on my television screen, I dared to believe God could do the same thing in the Muslim world. If it could happen in Poland, East Germany, Romania, Albania, Bulgaria, Hungary – even the great colossus of Russia – faith grew in my heart that the spiritual wall between Muslims and Christians could also be brought down. Not through gulf wars or joining the fight against terrorism, but calling upon the living God to act sovereignly, as he did when the Iron Curtain came down.

I know why the Iron Curtain fell. I heard the reason from the lips of a young lady named Joanie Herwig. In a prayer meeting for the events that were happening in Communist lands in 1989, Joanie stood and said, 'I have never told anyone this before, but I just have to tell someone! I was afraid people would think I was crazy! I have prayed for years that all the governments of Eastern Europe would collapse all at once, so the whole world's attention would be drawn to Eastern Europe and everyone would know that God did it!'

Pointing at the Bible, Joanie exclaimed, 'Look, here are the promises God gave me. He promised me that all the Communist governments would fall at the same time.' Pointing at her Bible, Joanie began sharing verse after verse the Lord had given her for each of the Communist nations. Joanie Herwig had apostolic passion. She rose above her personal needs, listened to God, and acted in obedience.

Apostolic passion must exceed political passion, or we end up fighting the wrong battles. Taking sides with Israel, or America, will not solve the problems of the Communist world or the Middle East. We must take God's side. It is not the kingdom of democracy we must preach, but God's kingdom of righteousness, joy and peace through Jesus Christ. When we live and pray and dedicate our lives to his purposes with passion, we are changed and God works through us.

Making covenant with God

I believe in making covenant with God. The Red Sea Covenant, as it came to be known, was just one of several covenants I have struck with the Lord in my lifetime. I realize this raises theological questions about the sovereignty of God, but my reading of the story of God inspires me to believe that God welcomes us to seek him and to make the longings of our hearts known to him. There is no question that God initiates covenants with those he calls. But he also welcomes us to initiate covenants with him. Jacob wrestled with the Lord until he responded. Gideon asked God for a 'fleece'. Jeremiah responded to the moving of God's Spirit in his heart and became a flaming spokesman for the Lord. Jeremiah was convinced that it was God who raised up kings and pulled them down. Jeremiah wrote these words:

> At any moment I may decide to pull up a people or a country by the roots and get rid of them. But if they repent of their wicked lives, I will . . . start over with them.[7]

It is the covenant-keeping mercy of God that both inspires and enables us to keep the covenants we make with him. The covenants I have made with God inspire me to keep going when my passion wanes. A covenant is like a marriage vow. It protects your commitment when romantic feelings fade.

---

[7] Jeremiah 18:7–8, *The Message*

Apostolic passion is the result of a covenant with God. It happens because we consciously dedicate ourselves to living radically and obediently for Jesus. It is not something that happens to us, but is the result of pressing into God for a set of core values that we will live or die for.

I don't know about you, but I don't seek fame or riches or security here on earth. In my weaker moments I may be tempted with those things, but what I want more than anything else is to leave a legacy of eternal influence on people's lives. I picture myself in heaven someday, bowing before Jesus and laying crowns at his feet. I picture those crowns as people I have had the privilege of influencing for Jesus while here on earth. I long to see the joy in Jesus' beautiful eyes on that day.

There is only one thing we can take to heaven besides our own hearts, and that is the people we bring to Christ. To that end, I have decided to invest my life in telling people about Jesus, and training other people to do the same. I want to pour my energy and time into a band of pioneers who lay down their lives for others. I want a heritage of spiritual sons and daughters who give their lives to see Jesus worshipped in places he has never been worshipped, in languages never heard in heaven.

This is my passion: I dream about people in remote corners of the earth having a church in their own language and culture. I dream about AIDS babies in Africa being loved and cared for by people who will give up their careers to care for the dying. I dream about thousands of university students in South Africa laying down their lives for those who have never had a chance to hear the name of Jesus one time, especially those who live under the heavy hand of oppression and injustice. I dream about Indian villages in Central and South America experiencing the justice of God, the forgiveness of their sins and the yoke of poverty lifted off them. I dream about reaching people in the Middle East and North Africa, in Tibet and North Korea and throughout the villages and cities of North India.

The church around the world is at a turning point, a place of opportunity where it can go in one direction or another. Though there has been tremendous growth in the *number* of followers of Jesus worldwide in the last 100 years, the overall *percentage* of Christians has not changed.[8] Every week the church in America loses another 53,000 people. The number of unchurched people in the United States who believe in God but don't believe in church has doubled in the last decade to almost 80 million people. Of the 400,000 evangelical churches in the United States, it is estimated that only 15 per cent of them are growing. No county in America has experienced a net growth of Christians in the last 15 years. While our profile as evangelicals grows in the media, the church is diminishing in size and influence on our culture. Yes, there are mega-churches that are growing, but overall we are losing ground.

> *Millions of Christians have given up on conventional church, not because the church demands too much from them, but because it demands too little.*

I'm convinced we need a new kind of Christianity, one that captures the hearts and minds of those outside the church walls and gives meaning to those inside those walls.

Millions of Christians have given up on conventional church, not because the church demands too much from them, but because it demands too little. The church in the West is stuck in a rut of building-based, Sunday-centric, pastor-oriented Christianity. If the experience of attending church on Sunday mornings boils down to sitting next to strangers for 1 to 2 hours, listening to another stranger (the pastor) talk for 30 to 40 minutes, and

---

[8] This observation is based on personal conversations with Todd Johnson, co-editor of the *World Christian Encyclopedia*.

then going home, it's no wonder 80 per cent of those who attend church are frustrated. That kind of Christianity puts immense pressure on pastors to perform and places great temptations on people to watch and criticize. Most Western Christians I know are bored with church. They are bored with it because many of their leaders are bored. The leaders are tired, overwhelmed by the expectations and demands placed on them. One young leader said to me recently, 'You don't need an M.Div to be a church leader, you need an MBA.' We are at a turning point in the church. The old way of doing things is not working. Something has to change.

The church was not placed on this planet to entertain people for one hour a week. The church was created by God to be the ongoing presence of his Son Jesus with skin on. The church was born for greatness. But when the church substitutes passion for God's glory with lesser passions, it is doomed to fail. That is why I believe apostolic passion is the missing dimension in much of the church today. God's response to terrorists and Islamic extremists, and to Christian fundamentalists, is the same. He calls all humankind to repent and turn to him. Jesus issues the same radical call today that he gave 2,000 years ago: 'Take up your cross and follow me!' This is the source of true passion. All other passions are imitations, mere replacements for the holy passion of God's love. I call this passion 'apostolic passion'.

The need for apostolic passion

What is apostolic passion? And why does it need to be restored to the church? The term 'passion' is used to describe everything from romance to hunger pangs. I don't know what it means to you, but for me passion means whatever a person is willing to suffer for. In fact, that's the root meaning of the word. It comes from the Latin *patior* and *passus*, meaning 'to suffer'. It is what you desire so intensely that you will sacrifice anything to have it.

Show me your cheque-book and your appointments calendar and I will tell you what your passions are.

The word 'apostle' means a sent one, a messenger. To be 'apostolic' means we are sent on a mission. The apostolic calling of the followers of Jesus includes forging new ways for *how* we do church and pioneering new places *where* we do church. To be apostolic is to be radical, to be adventurous.

'Apostolic passion', therefore, is a deliberate choice to live very intentionally for Jesus among our neighbours and in the nations. It has to do with being committed to the point of rejection or death to spreading the message of his love. It's the quality of those who are on fire for Jesus, who dream of making disciples for him.

God is on a mission, and all those who line up their vocations and passions to join him on his mission are *apostolic*. I will define the terms 'apostle' and 'apostolic' in more depth in the next chapter, but for now let me clarify that this word is not about titles and positions. Apostolic passion is about embracing the redemptive mission of God to this planet – through the church – starting where you live but extending to all nations.

> *God is on a mission, and all those who line up their vocations and passions to join him on his mission are apostolic.*

When apostolic passion has died in your heart

I know when apostolic passion has died in my heart. It happens when I don't spend time alone with Jesus dreaming of the time he will be worshipped in every part of the city I live in, and every part of the planet I live on. I know it's missing from my life when I sing about heaven, but live as if earth is my home. Apostolic passion is dead in my heart when I dream more about sports, toys, places to go and people to see, than I do about every nation in the earth and every neighbourhood in my city worshipping Jesus.

I have lost it, too, when I make decisions based on the danger involved in the assignment God gives me, not the glory God will get from me obeying him. Those who have apostolic passion are planning to go, but willing to stay. They want to go somewhere with and for God. You know you have lost your passion when you are deeply relieved that God does not send you to a remote tribe or foreign nation.

If you will not suffer and sacrifice for something, you are not passionate about it. If you say you will do anything for Jesus, but you don't sacrifice or suffer for him, then you aren't really passionate about him and his purposes. You have lost it. Apostolic passion is your inheritance, but you have to fight to possess it.

If you don't have it, how do you go about getting this thing called apostolic passion? Is it like ordering pizza at the door in 30 minutes or less, guaranteed? Is there an 0800 number to call? Or better yet, just 'send us your special gift of £15 or more, and we'll rush you some passion, express delivery, overnight mail'? I don't presume that I have all the answers about apostolic passion, but I have found some answers, and I feel compelled by God to share them with you.

I am motivated by reading how the apostle Paul got apostolic passion and what he did to keep it. It began for him with a revelation of Jesus that he nurtured all his adult life. Paul not only encountered Christ on the road to Damascus, he kept on seeing Jesus every day. This revelation of Jesus, and the revelation of God's purposes that came as a result, gave birth to Paul's passion. Knowing Jesus and making him known consumed the rest of Paul's life. By comparison, everything else in his life was dung, garbage, and religious trash.

> *Paul not only encountered Christ on the road to Damascus, he kept on seeing Jesus every day. This ... gave birth to Paul's passion.*

Nothing less will do for you if you want apostolic passion. If you are not willing to fast for it, give up sleep for it, suffer for it, and spend time with people who don't follow Jesus, you will never find it.

Do you want this thing called apostolic passion? Are you willing to pay any price to have it? I hope this book awakens something in you – but then the time for action comes. Apostolic passion will cost you meals fasted, nights spent driving and walking the streets of your city, crying out to God. It may take you to distant lands and will fill you with a vision of God's glory that will rock your world and the world of those around you.

When you find it, it will be because you have seen Jesus, and savoured him, and then discovered you cannot keep him to yourself. All those who are passionate for Jesus are passionate for what Jesus is passionate for. Jesus longs for one thing above all others, and that is his sweet presence to fill the earth. When you experience God's passion for his own glory, you will weep because of a vision of the Lamb glorified in all nations. When that happens you will be all too ready to do anything he calls you to do. Only read further if that is what you want and that is what you are willing to live for – and if necessary, die for. Human enthusiasm cannot sustain apostolic passion. When God invests his own passion in you, you must build and develop what God has given you.

Choosing your passions

We were created to be passionate. That is why worship is so vital to us – we were made to love God with pleasure and passion. God has placed within us a profound capacity for caring and enjoying. It is this capacity that allows us to worship God with feeling and devotion. And it is the same ability that allows us to give our selves with abandon to God. When God placed Adam and Eve in the garden, they loved the garden. There was an extravagant pleasure they received from naming the animals and tending the garden. When they walked with God, it stirred their hearts with intense love for the Creator. Sadly, sin entered the picture and Adam and Eve lost their original passion. The capacity was still there, but it was diminished under the heavy weight of sin and shame.

The capacity God gave Adam and Eve for passion is restored to each of us when we are regenerated by God's Spirit. It is that passion that the church desperately needs. It is not passion for passion's sake. It is passion with a purpose. God gave Adam and Eve the mandate to take dominion over the whole earth. He told them to be fruitful and multiply and fill the earth. That didn't mean just making babies. It was a call to join God in his plan to fill the earth with his glory by filling it with people who love him, people who permeate every dimension of society and every nation on earth.

God did not intend the Garden of Eden to be a little back garden in a remote corner of the Middle East. He planned for the whole planet to be a garden of pleasure and purpose. He gave Adam and Eve a beginning point, a place to start, but his plan was for them to expand the garden, to build and develop it under his direction and counsel. He wanted them to share in creating it with him, as it says in the book of Genesis:

Prosper! Reproduce! Fill Earth! Take charge![9]

God was giving them an invitation to join him in filling the earth with meaning and beauty.

Years later, God repeated this mandate to Abraham. He gave him a vision of the role he would play in building something great in the earth. He told Abraham that he would bless him and make his name great by making him the father of a nation, which in turn would bless all the nations of the earth.[10] This call to Abraham

---

[9] Genesis 1:28 ff., *The Message*   [10] Genesis 12:1–3

stirred passion in him. It is that passion that comes alive in us when we say yes to Jesus. Do you remember the zeal that burned in you when you first came to faith in Christ? But just as it can be lost, it can also be found and renewed.

Actually, apostolic passion is a set of passions. The wrong core values, or passions, can drain us of the passion God creates in us. We were re-born with passion in our souls. That passion has to be sustained, or it will be snuffed out.

In this context, I use the terms 'core values' and 'passions' interchangeably because a value is what we are passionate about, what we believe in at the deepest level of our being. Core values can be good or bad, actual or aspirational.[11] They can be conscious or unconscious in our lives. Core values can be chosen, but they are most often simply absorbed without our being consciously aware of what we are doing.

I define a core value as an inner belief. It is what the Bible refers to as the 'heart'.[12] Core values determine what a person truly believes and because of that, how they behave. Our core values are fashioned from five different sources:

1. Life experiences – Good and bad experiences lead us to value certain things more than others in life. Repeated responses and choices in life lead to deep-set patterns of believing, and become a person's values.

2. Self-interest – The human heart is capable of incredible selfishness. The Bible calls this sin. Sin is not just something we inherit, it is choices we make to sin against God.

---

[11] An aspirational core value is one we aspire to but have not integrated into how we think and behave. It is not wrong to aspire to certain core values, but it is challenging to change core values.

[12] For further study on the heart as the seat of our core values/passions, see Genesis 6:5–6; Joshua 14:8; Judges 5:15; 1 Samuel 9:19; 12:20; 17:32; Psalm 108:1; 109:22; 119:10–11, 32; 139:23; Proverbs 3:5; 14:13; 22:11, 17; 23:7; Obadiah 3; Luke 24:25; Acts 2:37; 4:32; 5:3; Romans 6:17; 1 Corinthians 14:25; Ephesians 4:18; Hebrews 3:10; 4:12; 10:22; 1 John 3:19–21.

3. Religious beliefs – What we are taught can and should influence what we believe and how we behave. It's possible to hold core values/passions in our heart that are incongruent with what we believe in our minds to be true. For example, we can believe in sacrificing for what we believe without actually living sacrificially.

4. Family upbringing – For good or bad, what our parents value influences what we value. Take a moment and reflect on some of the good or bad values that were handed down to you by your parents.

5. Our culture – Every culture has a set of core values that form the worldview of that culture. As an insightful learning exercise, make a list of the core values of your culture, and then compare them to the things Jesus valued. Put the list side by side to see the differences – or similarities.

If we do not change unbiblical core values to biblical core values, we will experience a 'core values conflict'. There will be a tension between what we believe and what we practise, between Jesus in us and the unbiblical values we have inherited from our upbringing and our culture. Unless this conflict is resolved through a 'values conversion', we will end up in a form of deception, saying we believe one thing and truly believing and practising another. In this case, it is possible that deception about our passions/core values will lead us to giving ungodly core values 'Christian' names to relieve the tension of believing one thing and living another. It's easier to adapt our lifestyle to our old values and yet call them Christian values.

This relieves us of the responsibility of changing how we live. This is why, for example, people call a life of extravagant selfishness 'God's blessing' and compromised standards of personal holiness 'Christian freedom'. Believing statements like 'God hasn't called me. . .' can be used to defend our lack of concern for the nations.

Three levels: hands, head, heart

Let me illustrate. We function on three levels in regard to our core values. Life is much more complex than this simple illustration, but it gets at a truth about how God designed us. Picture yourself on three levels:

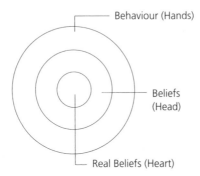

In order to foster apostolic passion we have to focus on our real beliefs – what we value – or the other two dimensions will just be behaviour modification and belief adjustment. It is necessary to change all three dimensions: our behaviour, our beliefs and our core values, but I have found the greatest challenge followers of Jesus face is a conflict between their 'real beliefs' i.e. their core values, and their new-found beliefs in making Jesus Lord. A person's behaviour will inevitably follow their core values. Behaviour flows naturally out of what we believe in our 'heart'.

The question naturally follows, 'How do I get my value system to sync up with my beliefs?' It is a process, but there are a few simple steps that will help bring about a 'values conversion'. Notice, I did not write 'easy steps' but 'simple'. Here they are:

Choose your passions

You may want to spend time studying the life of Jesus or Paul's missionary journeys to choose your passions. When I went through this process I wrote the word 'passion' by the actions or teaching of Jesus or Paul in the margins of my Bible to focus my thinking on what I thought were the values behind their actions. I consciously chose a few passions from my studies. My tendency is to be impulsive when I make commitments to the Lord, so I wanted to do this differently. I wanted to prayerfully focus on a few values and really live them. I suggest you don't choose more than three of four biblical core values to focus on at one season in your life. Once you make your choice, select a few Bible verses to reinforce them. Meditate on them to reinforce why they are important to you. Write them into your personal mission state- ment. Record them in your journal. Pray through them on a reg- ular basis. Choose them and re-choose them many times. We take a lifetime to develop unbiblical passions, so we shouldn't hold back from spending time choosing and nurturing apostolic core values.

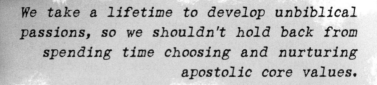

We take a lifetime to develop unbiblical passions, so we shouldn't hold back from spending time choosing and nurturing apostolic core values.

Nurture your passions

There is a battle for your passions. Choosing your passions is an act of spiritual warfare. If your passions are not greater than those of people in the world, you will be the slave of other people's pas- sions. Carefully decide what books you read, what films and TV programmes you watch, which people you hang out with, what activities you engage in – all to feed your passions. Your passions are like a wood fire: you have to continually add fuel to keep the fire going. I choose books and people and churches and out- reaches and activities – all with a view of keeping my passions at a high level in my life. I say this out of experience: you can lose your passions. I lost mine at one point while living back in the States. I found myself breathing air filtered through a poisoned belief system.

> *There is a spiritual battle raging for your passions. A few wrong choices and you can lose what it took years to build up.*

There is a spiritual battle raging for your passions. A few wrong choices and you can lose what it took years to build up. The way our culture influences us, you don't even have to choose to be 'worldly' – just go with the flow. Just be a person who merges with the crowd, and before long, you will have nothing inside you to motivate you to live passionately for God. If you don't nurture your passions, you can be compromised without making a conscious choice to forfeit lordship of your heart to someone else.

Focus your passions

Spiritual passion is not an end in itself. Our passions are in our heart to empower us to live for God's glory. They are to empower us to live obedient and godly lives. Focus your passions on what God is passionate about:

○ *Focus your passions on enjoying God.* God exults in his own greatness. The Bible refers to this as the glory of God. Worship him. Make lists of his attributes. Cultivate a life of inner pleasure focused on the beauty and goodness of God. Study his character. Read the word daily. Develop spiritual disciplines of prayer, intercession, meditation, spiritual warfare and worship.
○ *Focus your passions on the word of God.* Read it devotionally. Read it with a goal in mind. Pray the word. Memorize it and repeat it. Read it through, book by book. Read at least five

chapters a day. Read and study the book of Acts – it is a book about passion and passionate people. The men and women of Acts lived with apostolic intent.

○ *Focus your passions on being loved by God.* It sounds strange, I know, but God delights in you, so give him undivided time to love you and encourage you. Take time daily to allow the Spirit of God to tell you again how loved you are by Father. Allow his Spirit to speak deep into your spirit that you are adopted and loved; do this so you live your life from a place of security and confidence. The person who knows they are loved by God is immune to the lure of the world and the temptation to perform for the approval of others.

○ *Focus your passions on loving those God loves.* Pray for people you already know who don't know Jesus. Make a deliberate effort to engage others around you. Make lists of people who don't have a personal relationship with Jesus. Pray for people as you meet them, or just after you leave them. Take prayer walks and as you do so, pray blessings on your neighbours. Pray for the goodness and kindness of God to come to people at work. Ask God to show you how much he loves them.

○ *Focus your passions on the nations.* Choose a nation or people group that desperately needs Jesus and pray for them. Focus on the poor and unreached of the world. Adopt an unreached people group.[13] Set aside one day a week in which you focus your prayer on one or two people groups (a people group is an indigenous people with a distinctive language or culture) that have not had much of an opportunity – if any – to hear about Jesus.

A number of years ago I lost my apostolic passion. I still loved Jesus. I wasn't overtly backsliding. But I allowed myself to get seduced by the comfort and convenience of Western culture and

---

[13] To learn more about adopting an unreached people group, visit the Adopt-a-People website at www.adoptapeople.com

slacked off from focusing on the passions of God's heart for the lost. I started worrying about future security. I got concerned, overly concerned, about what would happen to Sally and me at the end of our lives. Slowly the American dream replaced the dream in my heart of God's glory filling the earth. I turned down invitations to speak in countries at war. I withdrew from some of the spiritual challenges I would have jumped at previously. It wasn't as if I chose to do those things, it just came naturally as a result of living in America. It's like being involved in chemical warfare. I was fighting an unseeable force that was dulling my spiritual focus.

> *Slowly the American dream replaced the dream in my heart of God's glory filling the earth.*

After a few years I faced what had happened in my heart. I accepted responsibility for my loss of apostolic passion. I repented openly before others. But the big breakthrough came when I chose to die to myself and the way of believing that had crept into my heart. I got on my knees and told God I would rather die a pauper with a heart of passion than have all America had to offer. It was a moment of death – and new life. I died to myself, and chose to follow Jesus where he led me. I got up from that time of prayer with my passion back!

> *I got on my knees and told God I would rather die a pauper with a heart of passion than have all America had to offer.*

It sounds a little simplistic, and maybe a little strange to say it this way, but I experienced a values conversion. I had had an evangelical mind, but I had allowed a Babylonian heart to capture me. I made a conscious choice to turn away from what had crept into my heart, and over a period of weeks and months, I chose five simple passions to be my core values. I chose these five because they are what stood out to me as I studied the words of Jesus and the life of Paul. These five passions stirred my desire to live for God's purposes in the earth, and continue to stir my heart today. They have been a touchstone for me every since.

Apostolic abandonment

Too many people want the fruit of the apostle Paul's ministry without paying the price that Paul paid. Paul died. He died to everything. He died daily. He was crucified with Christ. This strong-willed, opinionated man knew that he must die to self. He knew that in his flesh, in himself apart from Jesus, there was no good thing. He realized he couldn't generate passion. So he died. He abandoned his life. He abandoned himself. He was crucified with Christ. He died daily. He reckoned himself to be dead to sin so he could be alive to God in Christ Jesus. Paul declared to the Galatians that he was dead to the world and the world was dead to him.[14] One translation says Paul had been 'set free from the stifling atmosphere of pleasing others and fitting into the little patterns that they dictate'.

We live in a world of competing passions. If we do not die like Paul, we will end up with other passions. It's possible to deceive ourselves into thinking we have biblical passions when, in reality, all we have done is held a little baptismal service and given our old passions new names. We have chosen apostolic passion only when our hearts long for Jesus to be worshipped by our neighbours and in the nations. When that passion beats in our hearts above all other passions, then we know we have exchanged our life for his.

---

[14] Galatians 6:14

May I encourage you, dear friend, to give up your life? If you are ready to exchange your passions for his, your life for the life he has planned for you, I challenge you to pray this prayer, a similar prayer to the one I prayed to get my passion back: 'Lord, be ruthless with me in convicting me of my selfish ambition and my lack of willingness to die to myself. By faith, I die today to everything that has distracted me and held me back from loving you with abandon and boldness. I exchange my old passions for passion for you and your purposes. I choose this day to live for your glory. Let me see what you see and feel what you feel for the lost of the world. Fill me at any cost with apostolic passion. Amen.'[15]

Apostolic focus

We have seen that one of the greatest enemies of apostolic passion is lack of focus. You can expend energy on all sorts of good ministries, and not get one step closer to living with apostolic intent. I don't have anything against all the projects and ministries done in God's name in the church. God's people do them, and I don't question their obedience to God. But the church has an apostolic calling, an apostolic mission. God has called us to live single-mindedly for Jesus. We must focus, or we won't obey.

Focus on what? Obeying Jesus. God wants a people for himself. Being busy for God without sharing God's passion for more worshippers for his Son is good religion, but it's not the mission of God. Everything we do must lead to making, gathering, teaching and baptizing more fully devoted followers of Jesus. Some people are under the illusion they need a special calling to tell people about Jesus. But that is not true. Whatever you do for Jesus must lead to this one thing: that Jesus has more worshippers who know, love and obey him. Call that what you will. I call it making disciples; other people call it church planting. If those

---

[15] See Romans 6:11

terms do not appeal to you, choose another. But make sure that above all things you do what he commanded us to do: go, teach, baptize and make disciples.

That is apostolic focus.

Apostolic praying

A young man in Bible school offered to help a well-known preacher years ago when he was ministering on the streets of New York City. The man of God asked him how much time he spent in prayer. The young student estimated about 20 minutes a day. The preacher told him, 'Go back, young man. Go back for a month and pray for two hours a day, every day for 30 days. When you've done that, come back. Come back, and I might consider turning you loose on the streets where there is murder, rape, violence and danger. If I sent you out now on 20 minutes a day, I'd be sending a soldier into battle without any weapons, and you would get killed.'

You can get into heaven, my friend, without a lot of prayer. You can have a one-minute quiet time every day and God will still love you. But don't expect to hear 'well done, good and faithful servant' on one-minute conversations with God. And you certainly can't make it on that kind of prayer life in the hard places where Jesus is not known or worshipped. Here's a challenge for you: read everything Paul says about prayer, then ask yourself, 'Am I prepared to pray like that?' In his various letters Paul said that he prayed 'night and day with tears . . . without ceasing . . . with thankfulness in the Spirit . . . I pray constantly . . . boldly . . . for godly sorrow . . . against the evil one.' If we want Paul's passion we need to pray as Paul prayed.

If we want Paul's passion we need to pray
as Paul prayed.

Apostolic decision-making

If you live without a vision of the glory of God flooding our planet, you are in danger of serving your own dreams of greatness as you wait to do 'the next thing' God tells you. There are too many over-fed, under-motivated Christians hiding behind the excuse that God has not spoken to them. They are waiting to hear voices or see dreams – all the while living to make money, to provide for their future, to dress well and have fun.

The apostle Paul was guided by his passions as well as the impressions of the Spirit. Acts 20 and 21 tell of his determination to go to Jerusalem despite his own personal anticipation of suffering, the warnings of true prophets, and the intense disapproval of his friends. Why would Paul go against his own intuition, let alone the urgings of prophets and weeping entreaties of close friends? He had cultivated a set of core values that guided his life. Everything he did was values-based. He had a revelation of greater priority, of a greater motivation: the glory of God, and that revelation shaped and defined his inner beliefs.

Apostolic decision-making starts with a fresh encounter with God, then leads to a burden for lost people. Most people ask the where-and-when questions without a revelation of God's glory burning in their hearts. Is it any wonder they never hear God say 'go!'? They have not cultivated a passion for the passions of God. Lesser desires are holding them captive.

Present your gifts, vocations and talents to the Lord. Press into God. Stay there until you long to go out in his name. Remain there and nurture the longing to see people come to know him and the earth bathed with his praise. Only then will you be able to trust your heart if you hear God say 'stay'. Only those who long to go, have the right to stay.

Apostolic courage

It doesn't take courage to be a critic. And it doesn't take courage to mistrust others. It doesn't take courage to build walls around your heart and let no one in. It certainly doesn't take courage to place impossible demands on God and then feel justified in your disobedience when God doesn't meet your demands. It doesn't take courage to refuse to share Jesus with our neighbours or refuse to travel to another country to expose your heart to poverty, AIDS and suffering in our world. All it takes to stay put is a bucket-load of excuses, or a misuse of God's grace. Why do we have to wait until we are called? What's wrong with volunteering? God won't be upset with us if we volunteer . . . he won't lean over the balcony of heaven and say, 'Hey, cut it out! You're messing up the "I call you, you don't call me" system.' Stir up courage in your heart and go for it! It is this radical way of looking at serving God that is at the heart of apostolic intentionality.

> *Why do we have to wait until we are called? What's wrong with volunteering?*

Courage is the quality of those who see the need in the world, have faced their fears, and chosen faith instead of fear. Courage is overcoming our struggles by facing down the lies of the enemy that have been holding us captive. Courage is not the absence of fear in the face of danger; it is the willingness to trust God in spite of danger. Courage is believing that God's grace is sufficient for every situation, and then acting on that belief. I am convinced that in myself I would deny God if I was persecuted. I am banking on the grace of God. That, to me, is courage.

I believe courage is not waiting for God to call you to go, it is stepping out in faith with the hope that he will call you, then trusting him to show you where to go. Courage is volunteering to be used by God in places he cannot find anyone else to go, knowing God doesn't punish volunteers but rewards them.

Courage is not waiting for something mystical to happen to us to make us obey God, it is stirring up our hearts to believe God. The Bible says Daniel 'stirred' up his courage. It tells us that Joseph of Arimathea 'took' courage. Courage does not come arbitrarily to the brave; it is taken hold of by the obedient. It is the reward of those who refuse to be prisoners of their fears, the lies of the enemy and the temptations of the world.

> *Courage does not come arbitrarily to the brave; it is taken hold of by the obedient.*

Earlier in this chapter I told you about the covenant a few friends and I made in the Sinai Desert. It was apostolic passion that led us to make that covenant. Let me tell you a little about what God did as a response. One of the couples who participated in the covenant, Steve and Liz, now oversee more than 600 full-time volunteers who have devoted their lives to sharing the love of Jesus with Muslims. Lynn Green spearheaded a massive reconciliation walk involving thousands of Christians who participated in a walk from France all the way to Turkey, then down through Syria to Jerusalem. The participants in the reconciliation walk spoke at every opportunity they had in mosques and synagogues. Untold healing took place in thousands of conversations along the way. The 'reconciliation walk' was in the headlines of countless newspapers and TV broadcasts along the way. Followers of Jesus repeatedly asked for forgiveness for the murder, rape and pillage that was done in the name of Jesus through the Crusades. Thousands upon thousands of Muslims saw the love of Jesus in action.

I participated in the reconciliation walk with a friend, Peter Iliyn. We met with a Muslim leader in a Central Asian nation. After explaining our great sorrow at what was done in the name of Jesus in the Crusades, we asked if we could pray for him. He agreed. We asked God for the full blessing of the covenant God made with Abraham and Ishmael to be given to his family and all those he led. After our payer time, we handed him a short written summary of what we shared with him. He studied it carefully, and then asked if we minded if he handed out copies of the statement to be read in the 5,000 mosques he oversaw in his country!

Another amazing and ongoing result of the covenant we made is the 30-day Ramadan prayer focus. After our desert gathering, I felt led to call Christians around the world to pray for Muslims during their month of fasting. We did this, not because we agree with Muslims or they agree with us, but because we agree with God's desire to bless Muslims. The purpose of the *30 Days of Prayer* as it came to be called, was to provide understanding of Islam, and to spread a message of Jesus' love. Today, a simple 30-day prayer guide is printed each year, one page for each day of Ramadan, assisting Christians to understand and know how to pray for Muslims. At last count, the prayer guide is printed annually in 45 languages. Twenty-five million Christians participate each year in the month-long prayer focus.[16]

> *I felt led to call Christians around the world to pray for Muslims during their month of fasting, not because we agree with Muslims or they agree with us, but because we agree with God's desire to bless Muslims.*

God is working in the Muslim world. He is stirring the hearts of countless Muslim men and women to follow Jesus. I have met them all over the world. They tell about seeing Jesus in dreams at night. They speak openly about being a 'Muslim follower of

---

[16] For more information about how to participate in the 30 Days of Prayer, go to www.30-days.net

Jesus'. They read the words of Jesus and tell others about him, at the risk of losing their lives. The wall that separates Muslims from knowing Jesus has not completely fallen yet, but it is starting to crack. Someday it will crumble, and when it does, I want to be there, not to dance on the rubble but to kneel at the feet of Jesus with Muslim brothers and sisters who love Jesus and have trusted him for the forgiveness of their sins.

Dangerous people

If you have apostolic passion, you are one of the most dangerous people on the planet. The world no longer rules your heart. You are no longer seduced by 'getting and gaining' the things of this world, but you are devoted to spreading and proclaiming the glory of God. You live as a pilgrim, unattached to the cares of life. You are not afraid of loss. You dare to believe you may be given the privilege of dying to spread his fame on the earth. The Father's passions have become your passions. You find your satisfaction and significance in him. You believe he is with you always, to the end of life itself. You are sold out to God, and you live for the Lamb. Satan fears you, and the angels applaud you.

Your greatest dream is that his name will be praised in languages never before heard in heaven, and among your neighbours here on earth. Your reward is the look of pure delight you anticipate seeing in his eyes when you bow at his feet and receive the just reward of his suffering: the worship of those you have brought to him.

Alone, you are dangerous, but you are very dangerous because you have chosen to pass on your passion to others . . . you threaten the demons of hell because you have apostolic intent. You deliberately pass on your passions to others. You are not satisfied with keeping it to yourself. That is the heart of everything we do in simple-church movements.

PART FIVE
Making Disciples

7

The Heart of Everything

Jesus started a movement. He modelled the values of the movement in the deliberate manner in which he selected and trained his disciples. Jesus started small and simple, but he had a worldwide movement in mind. It was a simple-church movement, begun with a band of nobodies who were turned into obedient disciples by being with Jesus. They learned his ways and advanced the kingdom of God by doing what Jesus did.

Jesus birthed and nurtured the organic movement he initiated without title or position. He did it by sowing the seed of the good news everywhere he went. He scattered that seed abundantly and indiscriminately in the soil of people's hearts, and then watched to see where the seed took root. As he went about sowing that seed, he looked for those who were hungry, and from those men and women he selected his disciples. From the good soil, he gathered a harvest.[1]

A careful reading of the first four books of the New Testament reveals a pattern that Jesus followed. He shared the good news with great numbers of people, encouraged them to follow him to learn more as he told them stories and did miracles, and then from those who were serious he raised up the future leaders who would take his movement to the nations.

---

[1] Mark 4:3 ff.

His way of making disciples was to select and focus on a few, ask them to join him as he reached out to people, then teach them in more depth what his stories meant and how the message applied to their lives.[2]

He spoke to the people of his day in a way that was relevant to their needs and desires. He spoke from inside their culture. Most of the people had given up hope for someone to save them from the crushing rule of the Romans: he told them the time was at hand for a new kingdom to be set up.[3] He talked as though he were starting a grass-roots revolution, which of course he was. He told them he had come to fulfil the promises of the prophets. There was a buzz about Jesus. 'Is this the one we are waiting for?' they asked.

All the while this was happening the disciples were watching and helping Jesus. They were part of something significant, even if they didn't fully comprehend what it was. Before his disciples were born again, Jesus was preparing them to be leaders in the organic, simple-church movement he began.

The Holy Spirit led Jesus, but Jesus also had a plan. He was not just spontaneously doing whatever came to mind that day. He was intentional. He carried out his plan from a whole different paradigm. If we want to birth movements and not just more meetings, we have to change our paradigm as well. Don't try to create a new wineskin and fill it with old wine. Don't rearrange the way you do worship services and call it a revolution.

Jesus bypassed the cumbersome religious structures and irrelevant worship practices of his day and started something living and organic. The word 'organic' is a good one to describe a spontaneously reproducing simple-church movement because it describes something that grows naturally, without artificial addi-

---

[2] Robert Coleman's classic book *The Master Plan of Evangelism* first made me aware of the principles Jesus followed to make disciples who would lead a worldwide movement.

[3] Mark 1:14–18

tives. It consists of elements that exist together in natural relationships that make growth and multiplication possible.

The word 'organic' is a good one to describe a spontaneously reproducing simple-church movement because it describes something that grows naturally, without artificial additives.

Notice the way Jesus got the disciples exercising gifts of leadership from the outset, before they were 'ready'. Jesus didn't wait for disciples to be born again, baptized, trained theologically, and supervised under a safe religious system with guaranteed controls before he was involving them in leadership. He got them out telling others about him within a few weeks of being with him.[4] He led the movement he began from underneath, very quickly involving the disciples in leadership assignments without mentioning positions or titles. He had a radically different paradigm from the religious leaders of his day – and of our day as well. He was training them to lead before they were actually born again, in our evangelical understanding of what that means. After all, the journey of discipleship doesn't start when a person comes to faith in Christ, but long before.

Jesus didn't wait for disciples to be born again, baptized, trained theologically, and supervised under a safe religious system with guaranteed controls before he was involving them in leadership.

By the way, have you ever asked yourself when the disciples actually were born again? Think of it this way: if you began a movement

---

[4] Matthew 10:1–14

now the same way Jesus got things going in his day, it would mean telling everyone you meet about Jesus, watching who responds with keen interest, and then selecting a few people who are most open, and investing lots of time in them. You would start to meet with this group of seekers in times of discussion over a meal. You would ask one of them to read a few short verses from the words of Jesus, another to lead a discussion about what Jesus meant and how his teaching applied to their lives, and still another to teach a new song they wrote.

> *Have you ever asked yourself when the disciples actually were born again?*

You would encourage them to tell their family and friends what they were learning about Jesus. You would meet in their homes, not yours. You would want as many of their friends and family to sit in on the discussions as possible. When you would come together as a group around a meal, you would model a facilitative style of leadership that got everyone involved, carefully taking a back seat so you could encourage their development. You would be pleased as they quickly took ownership of what was happening.

You would have already met one-on-one with your disciples behind the scenes, asking different ones to take part in the group gatherings. You would ask each member of the group to help make it happen in different ways, and then you would coach them, seeking to instil in them leadership values that would prepare them to lead new communities as they sprang up. You would encourage them to gather their friends and family members and tell them about Jesus.

To illustrate how a simple-church movement is much more organic and natural than we normally think, I want to tell you an amusing but amazing story about a friend of mine who worked among Muslims in North Africa. My friend Carlos related to me an incident about a Muslim friend called Ishmael who was very upset when he heard some mutual friends had got together at Carlos' home for a meal, and he was not invited. What Ishmael did not know was that Carlos was meeting with his church-planting team to talk and pray about how to share Jesus with Muslims. Not exactly the kind of meeting you invite your Muslim friends to be part of.

When Carlos heard the anguish in Ishmael's voice, he decided to ask him to join the team meeting the following week. He knew there was no way he could keep having his fellow team members come to his home for a meal and not invite Ishmael to join them.

So the following week, there was Ishmael having a good time with everyone, not knowing he had crashed a church-planting team meeting! They carried on with what they normally did: fellowship around a meal, prayers of blessing for the people of the land, worship, and time spent studying the words of Jesus from the Sermon on the Mount.

When Carlos observed how much Ishmael enjoyed being with them, he decided to ask him to read from the Sermon on the Mount and lead the discussion the following week. 'What will I say to them?' asked Ishmael with his mouth open. 'Would you like me to meet with you this week and we talk about it together?' Carlos asked.

At the appointed time, there was Ishmael, a Muslim, 'leading' a group of church planters in a Bible study group!

They met the following week to discuss the teachings of Jesus in Matthew 6 and 7. A few days later, at the appointed time, there was Ishmael, a Muslim, 'leading' a group of church planters in a Bible study group! Not just Christians, but church planters! It went well. It drew Ishmael deeper into the circle of friends, gave others an opportunity to learn about the importance of hospitality

in their host culture, and taught everyone that making disciples
the way Jesus did it is radically different from how we are taught
today.

Centred set or bounded set?

One of the big lessons we learn from this story, is to think differently about what church is and how people become part of it. It
is just as much a family to belong to, as it is a set of beliefs to
adhere to. We tend to think of people coming to faith in Jesus at
a specific moment on the timeline of their life, through believing
a set of doctrines, but my observation is that, for many people,
salvation is more of a process than a specific moment. And it is as
much about belonging as believing. For them it is more about
getting to know and trust a person – Jesus – than a big 'wow'.
For some there is a moment of crisis, but that is normally one step
in a journey with many stops and starts along the way.

If that is true, the sociological paradigm called the 'bounded
set' does not apply well to inviting people to know Jesus. The
bounded-set paradigm describes how we determine if people are
'one of us'. There are ways we know if people are either 'in' or
'out'. We may determine this by the colour of their skin, their
ancestry, the language they speak, the clothes they wear, the
food they eat, or the way they think and act. Every culture, and
most sub-cultures for that matter, have ways of determining who
is part of their group.

The bounded-set paradigm is handy for deciding if a person is
Korean or an airline pilot, but not whether they are a true follower of Christ. I like to know for sure the pilot of the plane I fly
in does more than just wear a pilot's uniform; I want to know that
they have been to pilot school, flown many hours, and are
proficient in their piloting skills. There is a place for knowing if
people are in or out of a group or subgroup of people.

But the bounded-set way of thinking does not work well when

it comes to being a disciple of Jesus. We need another way of seeing. Appearances can fool us. Some people look close to Jesus when their hearts are in fact far from him. And there are others who are very devoted followers of Jesus and may not 'look like a Christian' but who have come to a place of faith in Jesus in their heart. They may dress or act or do things that many followers of Jesus do not do, but that does not mean they are not sincere.

This way of belonging to a group is what is called the 'centred set' and is all about believing a set of values or being devoted to a person who stands at the centre. The boundaries are fuzzy in terms of who is 'in' or 'out', but the centre is clear: devotion and obedience to the person of Jesus Christ.

If we are going to radically change the way we do church, it will mean being among the people who have not yet placed their trust in Jesus. Just as it was not always clear who was or was not yet a disciple of Jesus among his followers, we will have the same 'messy' boundaries if we are effectively doing church with our neighbours and non-Christian friends. Different people are at different places on their road of seeking to know the truth. But if the centre is clear – Jesus – we can be focused on making disciples who love and obey Jesus.

One youth pastor who grasped these principles said to me, 'Floyd, there are young people in our youth group who are supposed believers but they don't have any spiritual hunger or seek Jesus; and then there are others who don't yet believe in Jesus, but are definitely seekers. We have believers who don't seek, and seekers who don't yet believe.' If we can live with unclear boundaries yet a clear centre, we have grasped the message Jesus was trying to convey about making disciples.

It is not about stepping across a man-made boundary of rules and practices, but inviting people to Jesus. Jesus offered nothing more than himself. He was the message. He invited men and women to follow him. The first disciples did not have the security of a religion to belong to or a set of rules to obey. They just had Jesus.

The first disciples did not have the security of a religion to belong to or a set of rules to obey. They just had Jesus.

Movements, not just meetings

These radical principles don't just apply to reaching Muslims and people in other cultures. They are being lived out in the so-called West – in South Africa, the United States and Britain. I have seen them at work in a bar in Pretoria, a 24-7 'boiler room' in Guildford, a shoe-store church in San Francisco, a group of students called The Underground in Tampa, and a 24-7 prayer community gathering in an art gallery in Kansas City.

Neil Cole describes his journey from a static kind of church-planting model to a dynamic and rapidly expanding organic movement of over 800 simple churches in his book, *Organic Church*.[5] Cole describes his journey of disenchantment with 'church growth' seminars that explained the secret to growing churches revolved around clean bathrooms and plenty of parking spaces. Cole comments, 'Apparently, the kingdom of God is held up by dirty toilets and poor parking. Jesus will have to wait for us to clean up our act. In India and China, however, where the church is growing fastest, among the most noticeable missing ingredients are clean toilets and parking spaces.'[6]

Cole describes coming to the realization that God wanted him to help birth a movement that radically lowered the bar for what it meant to be church, but raised the bar for what it meant to be a disciple in the church. By aggressively sharing Christ and making disciples, their movement, Church Multiplication Associates (CMA), grew in just a few years to over 800 churches in more than 30 states in America, and 25 countries around the world.

---

[5] Neil Cole, *Organic Church*.   [6] *Ibid*, p 94.

God wanted him to help birth a movement that radically lowered the bar for what it meant to be church, but raised the bar for what it meant to be a disciple in the church.

How does such a movement happen? There has to be the blessing of God, for sure. But besides that, simple-church movements are spurred in their growth by personal discipleship. It is people discipling people. Programmes don't disciple people, buildings don't disciple people . . . *people disciple people.*

It is the heart of what we do in our own movement. In Cape Town, I meet with Nelis weekly, who in turn disciples Timothy, who meets several times a week with three young men, and if they trust Christ, Timothy will train them to reach others also. In Pretoria, it was Gawie who discipled Cobus and Marlize, who in turned discipled Gustaf and Marina, Frans, and Werner, who are now leading the simple church. Cobus and Marlize are now in the Middle East, where their dream is to build a movement of simple, reproducing communities carried forward through disciple-making relationships.

In South Asia, it is Bob and Sonam pouring their lives into the new leaders of a simple church of believers from Hindu and Buddhist backgrounds, who in turn are making disciples of family members and neighbours, who are discipling others as they put their faith in Christ.

I could tell the same story over and over again: Danny discipled Jaku who discipled Raymond who is discipling the leaders of 15 simple churches, and dreams about them reproducing throughout the Ndebele people in Limpopo province in South Africa – and beyond.

What is at the heart of everything we do?

Jesus said the parable of the sower gets at the heart of everything we do. Notice how important Jesus ranks this parable in all of his teaching:

> But if you can't understand this story, how will you understand all the others I am going to tell?[7]

This story strikes at the heart of what Jesus modelled for his disciples, and what he expects of us today. He sowed the seed indiscriminately and abundantly in all the towns and villages of Galilee. He said there were going to be four responses: callousness – the hard ground; quick acceptance without depth – the shallow, stony soil; those who respond but then are caught up in the cares of the world – the thorny ground; and those who respond with depth and sincerity – the soft soil.

Here is what I learned a long time ago about disciple-making: look for those who are genuinely open and want to grow, and invest lots of time and energy in them. I learned that I am not responsible for making people grow who don't want to grow. I love them and pray for them, but I don't chase after them. I continue to love them and serve them while I look for those who are serious about knowing and obeying Jesus.

In our church-planting endeavours in Cape Town, we stress the loving invitation of Jesus to everyone, and then teach the loving commands of Jesus to those who are serious. We lower the bar for doing church so everyone can be part of it, and we raise the bar for being a disciple so everyone knows what it means to be a disciple of Jesus. We work hard at sharing Jesus with everyone we can, but give special attention to those who respond. Of the three kinds of soil that received the seed in the parable of the sower, only one kind was deep and lasting. That is what we look for to make our disciples, and our future leaders of simple churches. We

---

[7] Mark 4:13, NLT

consciously and unconditionally love all those we minister to, but we also recognize that some people are hungry to learn more about Jesus and some people aren't. We reach out to HIV-impacted children and take care of them, teach job and life skills to the poor, run sports programmes for all the youth who want to participate. But loving people unconditionally and making disciples are two different things. If we don't make a distinction, we will confuse the great commandment to love our neighbour as ourself, and the great commission to make disciples of all nations.

*Loving people **unconditionally and making disciples** are two different things.*

Formation not just information

It's been the same in my own life. When I think about who has influenced me most, it's the few people who made a significant investment in me. These are men and women who believed in me and took time to impart to me what God had deposited in their lives. God used them to form my life. The goal of discipleship is not disseminating information, but life-on-life formation. I have heard a lot of great sermons in my days. I have read many excellent books. And I have interacted with world-class leaders. But what really changed my life were those who took the time to get to know me and mentor me. Those are the ones who really impacted me. I can count them on two hands. God put something in each of them that was unique, and they passed it on to me. I am what I am today because of these men and women.

People like Gordon Fee. Dr Fee was one of my professors while studying at Vanguard University. He was much more than a professor actually – he became a mentor. He taught me about grace, the kingdom of God, and the incarnation as a model for mission and life. He made the Gospel of John come alive to me. Though tough as nails academically, I looked forward eagerly to my classes with Dr Fee. His style was to lecture for the first half of the class, and then inevitably he would push back his notes, stand, get teary eyed as he allowed the Bible text we were studying that day to touch his heart, and he would preach to us. He would drive home the meaning of the text we were studying with tremendous passion and anointing. Though there were only 10 to 15 students at a time in most of his classes, he preached to us as though we were thousands. On many occasions our class times would end up in a prayer time as we responded to the message we had just heard.

Dr Gordon Fee, scholar, professor, author and prophetic preacher, became a friend. He took time to hear my story. He would come by my room in the resident hall to visit me and the other students. He would stop by the gym and shoot hoops with us as we practised for our next game. He invited me to his office to chat. He poked around in my heart when he sensed I was not doing well. There has never been a time I have preached God's word that I was not passing on to others what was imparted to me by this man of God. After I completed my studies, Gordon and Maudine supported Sally and me financially for more than 25 years. He visited us in Afghanistan and Amsterdam. He has remained a friend all our lives.

And then there was Pop Jenkins. Pop was a Sunday school teacher from Fresno, California. He would travel six to seven hours south to the university campus in southern California where I studied to seek out those students he felt led to disciple. He would wander the campus, looking for someone to spend time with. I had heard about this short, roly-poly, odd little man who hung around campus, but had not met him until one day he came up to me in the 'stacks', the study desks hidden away in the back of the university library. His introduction was rather odd. After asking if I was Floyd McClung, he simply said, 'God has sent me to be a doormat in your life. God wants me to serve you.'

Pop Jenkins burned with one consuming passion, and that was to inspire young men to love the nations. He had one calling, and that was to mentor one or two students at a time to receive God's love for those who had never heard the name of Jesus. Pop and I walked the campus and talked for hours about missions. It was Pop Jenkins who took me on my first short-term missions trip. It was with Pop Jenkins and my younger brother, Alan, that I took my first missions trip outside the United States. We headed south in my 1947 Plymouth. We visited San Felipe, a small fishing village in the Gulf of Mexico. It was only a few days of outreach, if you can call it that, but it turned my world upside down. Pop Jenkins passed on a level of compassion I had never experienced before. Most of that trip, my brother and I watched Pop Jenkins weep for people. One old man, two young boys, and a few days in Mexico. But it up-ended my world.

Sam Shellhammer taught me the value of a daily time with Jesus. I met Sam during my first year at university. I was fixated on sports and girls. Sam stopped by one morning, introduced himself, and asked if I would like to meet with him on a daily basis for devotions. When I asked him when we would meet, he said 5.30. At that stage in life, I thought 5.30 only happened once a day. I looked at Sam like he was crazy, but I couldn't resist him as he stood there with a big grin on his face. I don't know why to this day I said yes, but I did. That was the beginning of a wonderful friendship. Sam often had to rouse me out of bed so we could pray together. But over time I learned the blessing of starting the day with Jesus. I didn't have the discipline of getting up on my own initiative, but I wouldn't break my commitment to Sam, so it became a way of life. Now, 40 years later, I cannot imagine starting the day without spending time with Jesus.

At that stage in life, I thought 5.30 only happened once a day.

I heard Loren Cunningham speak the first time in a mandatory chapel service in my second year at university. Chapel times were

normally boring, but not this day. I sat spellbound from his open-
ing words. Loren quoted Matthew 5:8, saying that only the pure
in heart would see Jesus. He explained that humanly speaking it
was impossible to evangelize the world, but if we would love God
with a pure heart and do the possible, God would do the impossible – through us. I was hooked. I signed up for an outreach over
Spring break that Loren was organizing in Las Vegas. I was 19
years old. I had just come back from Mexico with Pop Jenkins and
was looking for a challenge. I got it from Loren, and then some.

God had given Loren a vision of waves of young people wash-
ing up on the shores of the world. Loren helped pioneer the concept of short-term missions, of young people being used by God
as they stepped out in faith to trust God for impossible things to
happen. God used Loren to impart a vision to me for every person on the earth being evangelized in one generation. I learned
to hear God's voice under his leadership, and was given the
opportunity to do what God told me to do when others said it
was impossible. Loren believes in people. Now 14,000 full-time
workers with Youth With A Mission and over a million volunteers
have proven that the principles that Loren teaches are true and
still work today.

There are others I could mention. Joy Dawson. Francis Schaef-
fer. Christy Wilson. Ken Wright. My father. God shapes our lives
through people. Everything God does is through people. It's the
principle of life-on-life impartation. He could use angels to
accomplish his work on earth, but he has chosen to work through
people. If we are to be all God wants us to be, we must find those
mentors that God has for us and receive from them, and in turn,
look for those God wants to impact through our lives. In 2 Samuel
it says about King David that he 'gathered the choice men and
women of Israel'.[8] Disciple-making is looking for those God has
selected for us to disciple and passing on what God has deposited

---

[8] 2 Samuel 6:1

in our lives. It is the heart of everything we do that counts for God.

> *Disciple-making is looking for those God has selected for us to disciple and passing on what God has deposited in our lives.*

It's the way Jesus did church

Jesus chose a few people and poured himself into them. He preached to the multitudes, but he spent most of his time with his disciples. Jesus calls us to follow his example by reproducing what he has given to us in others, who in turn are to invest in others also.[9] Building a disciple-making culture and birthing a disciple-making movement does not happen by accident. Passionate people catch the fire that burns in them from someone else and in turn pass it on to others. Every person who is influencing other people's lives can tell you about the people who impacted them.

There are churches and movements today that produce these kinds of results, while others don't even come close. The reason? Some have caught the vision of relational disciple-making, and others have not. How can we expect to reproduce our lives in others, if we don't deliberately pass on to them what God has given us?

There is a valley of dry bones God wants to use, but those bones won't become an army until they are prophesied over. The dry bones are the poor, the rebellious, the marginalized of society, the broken, the young and – if they are willing to humble themselves – the rich and powerful. For the dry bones to live again there has to be desperation for change. The dry bones are

---

[9] 2 Timothy 2:2

those people longing for someone to believe in them. They carry wounds, have been abused, suffer from AIDS, are widows and single parents, they look scraggly and are often so poor they have lost hope of finding a purpose in life.

For the dry bones to live again there has to be desperation for change.

Anything good in our life is the result of us being impacted by someone else. It began with Jesus and his disciples 2,000 years ago, and it carries on with us today. If you have hope, passion, a sense of purpose and destiny, it is because you received it from someone else. You are one of many in a long line of people who have touched each other's lives. And if others are changed because of you, it will be because you gave to them what has been given to you. Passion for Jesus and his purposes in the earth is received, nurtured, then passed on to others. That's how it lives on in the church. That's how God raises up an army from dry bones.

Rice Broocks, in his book, *Every Nation in Our Generation*, says we can raise up men and women today who have just as much potential for apostolic anointing and passion as Paul, even more than Paul.[10] How? Through the seed of Jesus, planted in us through another believer. Jesus said those who believe in him and the works he did, they will do also – even greater works than he did.[11] This promise is not a blanket guarantee for anyone who aspires to make a difference in the world. There are conditions for receiving such passion and purpose. Just hours before he went to the cross, Jesus spelled out those conditions:

> I say to you, unless a grain of wheat falls into the ground and dies, it remains alone; but if it dies, it produces much grain. He who loves his

---

[10] Rice Broocks, *Every Nation in Our Generation*, Creation House 2002, p 99.
[11] John 14:12

life will lose it, and he who hates his life in this world will keep it for eternal life. If anyone serves me, let him follow me...[12]

Jesus is the grain that fell to the ground and died. Those who have loved and obeyed him down through the centuries are the disciples of Jesus, the new grain that his seed produces. But notice the qualifier: these disciples of Jesus are people who have lost their lives. They have died to the cares of the world. They have taken up their cross, followed Jesus, and are devoted to obeying him with singleness of mind and heart. They have exchanged their old life for the new life Jesus gives them. They do simple church throughout the week. They have courageously chosen to reach out to a few others and invest in their lives. They are faithfully and fiercely focused on obeying Jesus' command to make disciples.

> **Passion and purpose come at no less a price than Jesus and his disciples paid to possess them.**

Passion and purpose come at no less a price than Jesus and his disciples paid to possess them. If Jesus walked the way of suffering to receive the blessing of the Father, do we think we can do anything less? If we are willing to align ourselves with a tribe of people with proven passion, it will mean getting out of our comfort zone, taking up our cross, and putting ourselves in harm's way for the sake of the gospel. If we are willing and obedient, we will experience the same fruit as the first disciples.

Jesus chose personal investment in people's lives as the primary way he did church. The Sunday-centric model of church will not change the world. Some think the church started on the day of Pentecost, but I disagree. Jesus led the first New Testament church. He modelled for us how to do church by the way he gathered and

---

12 John 12:23–26

invested in the lives of a few men and women. He modelled a new way of doing church. He gathered, equipped and mobilized faithful men and women into a movement of devoted followers.[13] This kind of one-on-one intentional relationship is the key to helping people get freed from their brokenness and turned on to serving Jesus. Discipleship isn't a school or programme, but a lifestyle of passion and purpose passed on through personal investment and involvement in one another's lives.[14]

Dry bones turned into an army

I met a young man a few years ago named Charles. Charles was 24 and had a dream. He was driving me to the airport after a recent visit I made to Antioch Community Church in Waco, Texas. I asked him if he had a dream, and he eagerly shared it with me. 'I want to have eight generations of disciples. I am an eighth-generation disciple, starting with Jimmy's brother,' referring to his pastor, Jimmy Seibert. 'I have traced it back through the guys in our church, starting about 20 years ago. It started with Jimmy's brother leading Jimmy to Jesus, Jimmy discipled Mark, who discipled Robert, and Robert discipled. . .' Charles named the men in the long chain of relationships that he knew by heart, and could articulate the principles that made it so powerful.

'My dream is to have eight generations of my own disciples – even more. I want to start a church-planting movement someday, and I know I won't be able to do it unless I invest my life in others.' Charles was right. There are no shortcuts to doing church the way Jesus did it. He built a team that became a community that multiplied and grew into a movement. It was Jimmy, Charles's pastor, who once said to me that it takes four generations of disciples over a period of about 20 years to birth a movement. You can

---

[13] Matthew 28:19–20; 2 Timothy 2:2

[14] 1 Thessalonians 2:18–19; 3:10

build a disciple-making church with two or three generations of disciples, but Charles was already dreaming of more than one church, and more than four generations of disciples. He wanted to build a church-planting movement, and he knew it had to begin with him leading people to Christ and investing in them one at a time.

I believe God wants to use every person to launch a disciple-making movement. Depending on a person's gifts and callings, some movements will be small and some large. All it takes is investing in a few people at a time. I encourage the All Nations church planters we train to dream big – but build small. My question is, why wouldn't we want to dream of impacting thousands of lives that do great things for God? God did not design the church to function without passion and purpose. He wants us to dream big, but the way to build something big is to start small, one person at a time. Everyone can disciple at least two or three people.

> *Everyone can disciple at least two or three people.*

When I quizzed Charles on what steps he was taking to turn his dream into a reality, he told me about room-mates he was reaching out to and new followers of Jesus he was meeting with weekly to teach to have a quiet time and share their faith. He was taking simple, practical steps to turn his dream into a reality. He was faithfully working away at it, and you know what? I believe him. I believe his dream will become a reality.

This same pattern is repeated throughout church history. One amazing example is a Sunday school teacher named Edward Kimball back in the 1880s. Kimball began to strike up a friendship with a few young men in his Sunday school class. Kimball was particularly committed to a fellow classmate fresh from the farmlands who had begun working in a nearby shoe shop. One day

Kimball decided to visit his new friend at work. He entered the shop, found him in the backroom, and struck up a conversation. Later he led his friend to a personal relationship with Jesus.

When describing this young man years later, Kimball said, 'I have met few friends whose minds were spiritually darker, or who seemed more unlikely ever to become a Christian. . .'[15] But Kimball's faith in his new friend, and his investment of time and personal mentoring, made a huge impact. His new friend was D. L. Moody, who went on to become an evangelist who led tens of thousands to Jesus. Eventually Moody invested in the life of a man he met in England, named F. B. Meyer. Meyer was a pastor who resisted Moody's evangelistic zeal and fiery preaching style, but responded when Moody invited him to the States to spend time together. Meyer was deeply impacted by Moody's personal life, more so than his preaching.

Meyer in turn influenced a man named J. Wilber Chapman who decided, as a result of his friendship with Meyer, to go into full-time evangelistic ministry. One of Chapman's disciples was a man named Billy Sunday. Sunday in turn spent time discipling a group of businessmen in North Carolina. After years of praying together, these men were prompted by God to invite an evangelist named Mordecai Ham to speak to a citywide gathering in Charlotte, North Carolina. During one of the meetings conducted by Ham, a young teenager came forward and gave his life to the Lord. His name was Billy Graham.

Edward Kimball started a chain reaction in 1880 that eventually reached the world's most influential evangelist, Billy Graham. By investing in a few people's lives, these men passed on to each other what had been given to them. They followed the example begun by Jesus when he spent time with a few young men many years before, pouring himself into their lives.

---

[15] Waylon Moore, *Multiplying Disciples: New Testament Method For Church Growth*, NavPress 1981, pp 16–17.

Discipleship defined

Discipleship is not telling other people what to do, nor is it a rigid set of rules and practices for spiritual growth. Nor is it a way of relating for 'moderns' that does not apply to 'postmoderns'. Here is a simple definition for discipleship: it is helping another person to know, love and obey Jesus.

> *Discipleship is helping another person to know, love and obey Jesus.*

Making disciples is deliberate. It's more than hanging out and hoping others 'catch it'. Personal discipleship happens as a result of encouragement and exhortation. It includes calling out the destiny of God in people's lives. It is accountability to others.

We are created by God to reproduce after our own kind. If we are proud and arrogant, we will produce the same fruit in others, and if we are humble and transparent, we will reproduce that as well. Paul said to the Corinthians:

Imitate me, just as I imitate Christ.[16]

To the Thessalonians Paul wrote:

You know how we lived among you for your sake. You became imitators of us and of the Lord . . . so you became a model to all the believers in Macedonia and Achaia.[17]

To produce that kind of spiritual fruit in others it's necessary to define what we are and are not responsible for. We have to set clear boundaries. Clear boundaries are maintained in discipling relationships by not taking responsibility for another person or in overriding them in matters of conscience. While discipleship involves helping each other grow in Christ, it doesn't mean we take responsibility for each other's decisions.

---

[16] 1 Corinthians 11:1   [17] 1 Thessalonians 1:5–7, NIV

People grow the most when they learn to hear God's voice for themselves. The aim of making disciples is to point people to Jesus. There is no greater joy for a person than when they discover God's will for themselves. As much as we may be tempted to give people the answers or 'fix them', God alone can transform the human heart. God has designed us to take hold of truth internally and then apply that truth to areas of our character that need changing. Every person must grasp God's truth for himself or herself and not look to others or external rules to follow. If we challenge someone about something we think is wrong in their lives, and they do not heed our advice, a patient, loving response will go much further than a demanding attitude.

> **People grow the most when they learn to hear God's voice for themselves.**

Getting serious about being a dry-bones army

As I have studied the great commission of Jesus as recorded by Matthew, I have concluded that Jesus had a very clear picture in mind of each succeeding generation of his disciples obeying him. Jesus said: 'Make disciples of all nations . . . teach them to observe all things I have commanded you...'[18] He commanded his disciples to make disciples as they went, baptizing and teaching. Then he told them to pass on this command to succeeding generations of disciples: 'What I command you, teach others also.' It couldn't be clearer.

I conclude five things from these words of Jesus:

Making disciples is not an option, it's a command

Jesus said, 'Teach them to observe all things I have commanded you.'[19] Obedient disciples make disciples. It's the heart of what

---

[18] Matthew 28:19–20   [19] *Ibid.*

we do. There is nothing more important than investing our lives in other people. There is no more crucial role for leaders in the church. When leaders invest their lives in other leaders, it's discipleship at it's best. Why? Because only those who live with apostolic intent can create a leadership culture conducive to attracting and releasing more leaders. When a leader develops other leaders, the impact of one life is multiplied many times over. It produces more fruit for the kingdom of God.

Making disciples is personal in nature but global in scope

Jesus said we are to make disciples of 'all nations'. It's God's way of spreading his glory to the whole earth. Personal discipleship connects us to God's global purposes. Nikolaus von Zinzendorf, the father of the Moravians, said:

> I have but one passion – it is He, it is He alone. The world is the field, and the field is the world; and henceforth that country shall be my home where I can be most used in winning souls for Christ.[20]

I want the same passion to burn in me, and in those I disciple. Don't you? Having a vision for the world is important for leaders who want to be leaders of leaders. Multiplication is not an end in itself. A world vision is about wanting God to be glorified in the whole world. It's about what God deserves.

Sally and I started praying together recently for unreached nations. We realized that to carry a passion for the nations we had to nurture apostolic passion in the place of prayer and intercession. We know we cannot pass it on to others if we are not carrying that passion deep in our inner being. We had become so caught up in church problems, so affected by them, that it was draining our passion. So we started praying together. And it has stirred passion in us, actually awakened the passion God had

---

[20] *Evangelical Mission Quarterly*, January 2002, p 371.

stirred in us previously, but was under a blanket of cares and disappointments. Now we have our passion back! We connected with God's heart for the lost, and recaptured our love for the nations.

Making disciples begins with building relationships with people who don't know Jesus

He directed his followers to 'make disciples of all the nations'. Jesus had people in mind who were not born again. His disciple-making started with those who did not know the Father's love. The word 'nations' in Matthew 28:19–20 is translated from the Greek word *ethne*, or literally, the 'ethnics'. Discipleship begins by reaching out to those individuals and peoples who don't know Jesus, and inviting them to follow him. That is particularly true for those who have never been evangelized.

Making disciples is another way of describing church planting[21]

How do we know this? Jesus commanded his disciples to baptize those who became his followers. Baptism is not just an act of personal obedience, it's a rite of passage into the global family of Jesus' followers. Baptism is intended to recognize and proclaim publicly that a person is following Jesus and is part of the fellowship of those who have made this commitment. Baptism declares that a person has been joined to the family of God. In most countries where disciples of Jesus are a minority, persecution doesn't begin until a person is baptized. Disciple-making does not

---

[21] The form, day and name is not important for how we do church, but following the biblical design for church is. Church is not a meeting on Sunday, but God's people gathering in his name for his glory. Church can happen any day of the week and in any place as long as people are gathering in his name for his purposes.

demand that we start new churches, but it certainly includes that. If we accept the simple definition of the church that Jesus intended for us, then gathering a few people and training them to love and obey Jesus is doing church the way Jesus defined it. Church in the home, the school, the office and any other place we can gather people is church in its simplest and most easily reproducible form.

Making disciples is God's way of transforming cities and nations

To quote Landa Cope, 'A reached community is not a discipled community.'[22] God uses the process of personal discipleship to bring about spiritual transformation in individuals' lives, and in turn, those transformed individuals influence their business, family, school and, in time, whole cities and nations. As Landa says, it is possible to evangelize people by the thousands and millions, but that does not mean they have been discipled.

Africa, the continent where we live, has actually been evangelized over and over again. But it has not been discipled. Africa desperately needs a new kind of Christian and a new way of doing church. When we disciple people in small groups, we are doing church the way Jesus did it. He modelled a new concept of church by gathering a few men and women and teaching them to love and obey him. In this sense Bill Hybels is right: the church is the hope of the world. Hybels declares:

> the church is the only God-anointed agency in society that stewards the transforming message of the love of Christ . . . the local church is the hope of the world.[23]

If the church is to steward the message in the same manner as Jesus, we must make disciples who know, love and *obey* Jesus.

---

[22] *Evangelical Mission Quarterly*, January 2002, p 99.
[23] Bill Hybels, *Courageous Leadership*, p 70.

That means every aspect of their life must be different: how they work, love their family, tell the truth, handle money with integrity, and reach out to the poor. Personal salvation is not enough. It is the beginning of a relationship with Jesus Christ, but if we follow the example of Jesus, calling people to obey Jesus is the goal. Discipleship is intended by God to lead to transformation, both on a personal level, and in the surrounding community. Sadly, many leaders are getting people to make decisions about Jesus but they are not making disciples for Jesus.

Sadly, many leaders are getting people to make decisions about Jesus but they are not making disciples for Jesus.

Weaving a discipleship net

When Jesus called Simon Peter and Andrew to become his disciples, he called them to be fishers of men. Later, he described the kingdom of God as being like a net that is cast into the sea to catch fish.[24] Though Jesus cared for individuals, he longed for *many* individuals to experience forgiveness of their sins. If we are to weave a net to catch the harvest God wants to bring through our lives, it means weaving a discipleship net. Weaving a net is another way of saying that God wants us to be intentional about winning and gathering and multiplying transformed people for him. In the same way that Jesus very deliberately selected and equipped men and women to bring in a great harvest, we're commissioned to do the same thing in our sphere of influence. Jesus did not come to establish an institution called church, but to empower people to do church intentionally. God has a passion to gather a great harvest for his glory – and he is inviting us to work with him as his co-labourers to draw in the net.

---

[24] Matthew 13:47

To weave an effective discipleship net means gathering and equipping people to be disciple-makers themselves. That means modelling disciple-making in our lives. It comes down to small groups and one-on-one times with people at work and school and who live close to us. If we select and faithfully disciple a few people in our sphere of influence, and they in turn are discipling others, we take the first steps to building a harvest-gathering net for the kingdom.

It begins with casting the vision, then inviting people to respond. Jesus began the process of training his disciples by letting them in on the big plans he had for their lives. He told them he was going to make them fishers of men. He told them, 'You will see heaven open.' Over and over again he encouraged them to dream big dreams for their lives, helping them catch a glimpse of the courageous men and women he was calling them to become. For those who were willing to obey him, he invested in their lives, then he asked them to disciple others.

You can do the same thing. Be on the lookout for those in your sphere of influence who are spiritually open. Start a Bible study group for anyone who wants to attend at work. Begin a family class for your neighbours. Or start a mums' Bible study group for the mothers in your neighbourhood. Get an open forum going on issues of justice at school or university. You'll be surprised who will attend. Reach out to those with a desire to know more, and when you find them, spend time with them.

Discipling someone means intentionally identifying with God's interests in that person's life.

Discipling someone means intentionally identifying with God's interests in that person's life. When someone says yes to your invitation to spend time together, get to know them – ask questions, draw them out, develop genuine interest in their lives. By prayerfully affirming them, you will impart life to them. Tell them God loves them. Pray for them. Bless them. Tell them the things God gives you for them when you pray for them, but don't use churchy language. Your encouragement and belief in them will give them courage to say yes to God's love. Help them realize the great value they have to God. Paul was doing this very thing when he wrote these words to his disciple, Timothy:

> I remind you to stir up the gift of God which is in you.[25]

Disciple-making movements

A major goal of Jesus' command to make disciples is a movement that will turn the world upside down. God wants his church to be part of a revolution. That means we can't just do church as usual. God wants us to reach the lost and empower each other to live for something greater than ourselves. George Eldon Ladd wrote:

> The church is the fellowship of disciples of Jesus who have received the life of the kingdom and are dedicated to the task of preaching the Gospel of the Kingdom in the world.[26]

This is what church is about. I realize it is easy to have big visions and not live them out. The Bible tells us why vision does not become a reality: it happens when we don't make disciples. According to my observation, a very small percentage of the efforts to evangelize the world have any kind of disciple-making value as part of their vision and mission.

We are guilty of asking too little of each other. We are created to serve God with passion, and passion is impossible without sacrifice. There is no way a city orchestra would allow a person to perform without practising, or a local sports team let kids play without practising. It's harder to become a member of some civic groups or sports clubs than most local churches!

---

[25] 2 Timothy 1:6

[26] George Eldon Ladd, *The Gospel of the Kingdom*, Eerdmans 1959.

We are guilty of asking too little of each other.

When Naaman came to Elisha and asked the prophet to perform a miracle and heal him of leprosy, Elisha gave him something to do, something that placed a demand on his pride and on his desire to receive a miraculous healing from God. Elisha asked him to dip in the muddy waters of the Jordan River seven times. Naaman expected a dramatic, personal miracle handed to him on a platter. He left angry, grumbling about the quality of ministry *he had not* received. This is a picture of the church that we don't want to be. But we're to do what Elisha did, and then some! We should ask each other to take big steps for God. We should not be reticent to ask for sacrifice. Like Elisha, when we ask people to obey the commands of Christ we are asking people to dip in the river. All we are doing is asking them to get healthy and freed up from their pride.[27]

When we ask people to be equipped to serve God, we are inviting them to dip in Naaman's river. It will set them free from false ideas of spirituality. They will experience cleansing from the leprosy of emotional brokenness and worldly values. Some may grumble about what we ask of them, but the hungry ones will be excited. If your key people go through a time of training and equipping, they're taking the steps we must all take to be part of a team, to join with others of like mind and spirit.

If we don't disciple the hearts and minds of people, someone else will do it for us. We live in a pluralistic culture. There is a constant battle for people's passion. Every disciple of Jesus is on the front line, frequently alone. Living in such an environment calls for clear biblical thinking and that means teaching and training. Memorized answers will not be enough. We must not let people think that by going to a meeting once a week they will be ready

---

[27] Adapted from Rice Broocks, *Every Nation in Our Generation*, page 10.

to face the challenges the enemy throws at them. Discipleship means engaging one another one on one all through the week. It means courses and workshops and prayer meetings that are aimed at equipping people to live as co-workers in spreading the good news of the kingdom.

If we don't disciple the hearts and minds of people, someone else will do it for us.

We have the awesome responsibility and opportunity to help shape the world-view of people and impart to them kingdom values. We are preparing front-line workers for the kingdom of God. God has called them, placed them where he wants them, and we get to equip them to be 'full time' for Jesus.

I told a large group of young professionals recently that I expected every one of them to go full time. That got their attention. Then I explained that I wanted them to make a decision. I told them their choice was not about whether they will be full time, but where they will be full time. They could do it in their job or in the nations. That is the choice: God wants all of us to step across an invisible line and decide to serve him first. Not our job, not the company, but Jesus. Then we can make a difference in our job and to our company.

The cost of discipleship

Jesus said that for those who believe in him, they will do greater works than he did. This promise is not a blanket guarantee for anyone who wants to be a disciple, but it is an insight into how much God wants to work through us. The cost is great, but if we are willing to pay the price, we will inherit the rewards of obeying Jesus. Paying the price means making a conscious decision to live full time for him at work, in our residence hall at university, with our neighbours, and to family members. It means dying to self, exchanging our life for his, confronting strongholds in our lives,[28] living a life of truth and accountability with two or three others on a weekly basis, and walking with others in honest, accountable relationships. God is calling us to father and mother movements of men and women who will do mighty exploits for God, and that will not happen if we are not diligent in seeking God and obeying him.

There are churches and movements today that produce these kinds of disciples, while others don't come close. The reason some churches and movements produce these kinds of disciples is because the leaders have been captured by a vision of laying down their lives for the purposes of God. If the people who lead have this kind of passion and vision, it will be passed on to others. Unless we make disciple-making our main agenda, all our visions are fantasy. It's the difference between dreaming and doing. And to do the job really well, we have to make our main business making disciples who make disciples.

Discipleship helps create a culture

When personal discipleship is a way of life for a church or movement, it ensures that what they stand for is passed on. Discipleship helps create a culture. One person cannot do that by themselves. A solitary individual cannot possibly be in enough places to influence enough people. By calling us to birth and nurture a disciple-making movement, God has designed a process that has the deepest impact on the greatest number of people. This is how a movement grows to impact thousands and even hundreds of thousands of people, all with the same passions and dreams.

Personal discipleship helps create the truest form of trust between people. Not just the kind of trust that believes a person

---

[28] 2 Corinthians 10:4–6

is reliable, but trust that is based on knowing that other people have our best interests in mind. It's the trust that comes from people baring their hearts to one another. It's the trust that results from dealing with conflict in healthy, loving ways. It's the trust that says, 'I want input from you, even if it means significant adjustment to my character or plans.'

Trust takes time, hard work, connecting from the heart, humility and lots of transparency. Trust is the assurance that you can rely on a person to tell you the truth, knowing that they believe in you. Trust creates safety, and assures others they can open their hearts to one another without fear of retribution. Without a strong sense of trust, people build walls, lift the drawbridge to their heart and live behind walls of suspicion and cynicism. Amazingly, we can pull down walls of mistrust through being vulnerable to another person. Discipleship embodies this way of relating.

> Without a strong sense of trust, people build walls, lift the drawbridge to their heart and live behind walls of suspicion and cynicism.

Discipleship is the difference

All kinds of programmes and strategies have been developed by Christian organizations and local churches to evangelize the world: mass crusades, seeker services, training programmes, creative outreaches, television and radio ministries, conferences, Christian music – on and on. All these programmes and strategies are great. But programmes and strategies don't disciple people. Great ideas don't make disciples. Disciples make disciples. There is no shortcut and there is no other way for a church or movement to reproduce itself.

Disciples make disciples. There is no shortcut and there is no other way for a church or movement to reproduce itself.

You won't reproduce the vision and values God has put in you if you don't make disciples. There is no other way to pass on the spiritual DNA God has put in you. There are many methods that seem more glamorous, and there are many approaches to ministry that get more attention. But if you want to build a leadership culture, if you want to impart apostolic passion to your church or movement, and if you want to see the gospel have its desired transforming effect on nations, it will happen because you make disciples.

How can we expect to reach the world, if we can't disciple people in our own back yard? How can we expect to touch nations and reach whole people groups, if we can't disciple the people around us? Disciple-making does not just make a difference, it is the difference. It is the Master's plan for world evangelization. It is God's way of transforming lives, families, towns, cities and nations. It is doing ministry just like Jesus. If you have great crowds to preach to, all the better, but remember, the crowds crucified Jesus. Having hundreds and thousands of followers is not a bad thing, but remember, when Jesus challenged those who followed him, many turned back. That's why the Son of God spent most of his time with a few men and women, pouring his life into them.

Take a moment if you will, and write down the names of those you have intentionally selected to disciple. Who are you investing your life in, right now? Have you told them? If not, don't let any more time slip by without doing so. Take them out for a meal or a cup of coffee, then take the risk, open your heart to them, and invite them to meet with you regularly. Outline what's on your heart. Cast your vision. Ask them to join you on the journey. Who knows, maybe the next Billy Graham or William Carey or Mother Teresa will be sitting across the table from you, longing for someone to recognize what's inside them, waiting for an invitation from God to live their dream.

To learn more about All Nations

visit

www.FloydandSally.org

or visit the All Nations website at

www.all-nations.info

You can also write to us at
P.O. Box 1661, Sun Valley 7985, Cape Town, South Africa.

Floyd and Sally live in Cape Town where they lead an outreach and training community. Their mission is to make disciples, train leaders and plant churches in Africa, Asia and other parts of the world.

Short-Term Teams
Each year outreach teams come to South Africa to work with All Nations in Cape Town. Contact All Nations to find out how your church or group can be involved.

Internships

An intern programme called SERVE is available if you are interested in receiving on-the-job training with All Nations. Interns serve from two months to two years, beginning each year in either June or January.

Discipleship and Leadership Training

Each year a six-month training programme called CPx begins the first weekend of February. Students from all over the world come for hands-on equipping to learn new ways of doing church and making disciples.

Teaching of the Month Club

In the near future Floyd will begin a 'teaching of the month' club. If you are interested in receiving messages on CD or downloadable mp3, contact allnationssa@gmail.com for more information.

To request information about how you can be involved in any of the opportunities described above, write to allnationssa@gmail.com for more information, or visit Floyd and Sally's personal website.

Appendix A

Five Practices to Plant and Multiply Simple Churches

I encourage people to follow these five practices for pioneering a simple-church-planting movement. They are not complicated, but that doesn't mean they are easy. Birthing new churches through holistic evangelism is always an act of spiritual warfare. When we bring good news and demonstrate real love to broken and lost people, we are invading the enemy's territory.

Pray

Pray alone. Pray as a team. Pray early in the morning. Fast and pray. Walk and pray. Spend half-nights in prayer. Pray to receive God's heart for people. Pray for discernment. Pray for passion and boldness. Pray for power. Pray for people to be set free. Pray with tears. Pray for workers. Pray for heaven to come to earth. Pray the Lord's prayer, phrase by phrase, as a guide for prayer. Expand on each phrase as you are led by the Holy Spirit:

- Worship – Our Father in heaven
- Consecration – Holy be your name
- Intercession – Your kingdom come, your will be done, on earth as it is in heaven. Give us this day our daily bread.

- Confession and forgiveness – Forgive us our trespasses as we forgive those who trespass against us
- Holy Spirit empowering – Lead us not into temptation
- Spiritual warfare – Deliver us from evil
- Commissioning and worship – For yours is the kingdom and the power and the glory for ever

Meet

Meet people and meet their needs. Ask people what their needs are, how they would like you to serve them. Don't come up with your own ideas and do it independently. Meet lots of people. In the first two weeks, meet only those who don't follow Jesus. In the first three months, set a goal of how many people you would like to meet, and then pursue relationship-building as your primary goal. If you are learning a language, meet with lots of people to practise what you are learning.

Sow the seed of the good news abundantly in people's hearts through sharing Jesus, disseminating appropriate portions of the Bible, and through prayer evangelism. Study the parable of the soils and the seeds in Mark 4. Reflect on how to recognize the four types of soil Jesus presents in this parable.

Disciple

As you meet people, discern who is spiritually open, and get to know them better. Select future leaders and invest major time and energy in their lives. Integrate practical ways of serving a person through sharing Jesus. Start Bible studies based on the words of Jesus, both his commands and his invitations. Select who you believe will be leaders in a simple-church movement and ask them to help you. Share vision with them of what you can see them doing to make a difference in their lives.

Take your future leaders with you when you visit other cities or towns to share Jesus. Welcome your disciples into your home and drop in to visit them where they live.

Gather

Start small and simple, with just a few people. Two or three is better than two or three thousand. Gather around food, Bible study, or discussions. Bring together a few of the people you are discipling so they get accustomed to sharing with others of like interest. As people come to faith in Jesus, involve them in taking part in the gatherings.

Build community with those you are gathering outside the gathering times. Stay in the background when you gather together. Deliberately develop a model of servant, behind-the-scenes leadership. Do this so there is no crisis when you give attention to other churches that are forming. Be a coach to a network of simple churches rather than an up-front leader to one larger community.

Multiply

Plan for multiplication from the time you begin. Think about how to plant the seeds for multiplication so it will happen naturally as the first group grows. Let it happen organically through burden rather than as a cold plan that is imposed by you. Pray with your group continually for the good news to be given to others. Discuss how to take the good news to those who have not heard. Make it a part of the DNA you impart to your disciples. Encourage them when they want to share with others, even when they don't fully understand what they believe. Trust the Holy Spirit in them to guide them.

Appendix B

Suggestions for Three-Person Accountability Groups

Personal accountability was never intended to be optional for disciples of Jesus. To intentionally develop a discipleship culture it is helpful to encourage people to meet in three-person accountability groups. As a movement grows it passes on its core values through such accountability groups. We call them Life Groups. Choose a name and go for it!

It's been said that if a group can hand down its core values from one generation to another for four successive generations, an unstoppable movement is born!

To facilitate the transfer of core values and genuine care for one another, I suggest the following guidelines for personal accountability:

1. Men and women meet separately.
2. Meet for an hour and no more.
3. Meet weekly.
4. Don't get sidetracked with lots of counselling.
5. Expect each other to be diligent and serious about personal growth and accountability.
6. Set growth goals and share them with each other for the following areas:

a. Prayer and reading the word
b. Sharing Christ with others
c. Character growth
d. Personal holiness and sexual purity
e. Discipling others
f. Passion levels
g. Finances

7. Divide the meeting into three parts:

   a. Check-in and follow-up
   b. Focus on the three core values of the kingdom of God as a basis for accountability
   c. Pray for each other and for those you are believing to come to faith in Christ

8. Focus on the seven commands of Christ:

   a. Repent, believe and be baptised
   b. Love God and others
   c. Share your resources and finances
   d. Forgive each other
   e. Pray and worship together
   f. Live a holy life
   g. Go and make disciples

Appendix C

The Three Core Values of the Kingdom

I have tried many approaches to helping people remember and focus on our core values. One thing is clear: a long list of core values will not be remembered or practised by anyone. I was inspired years ago by Jimmy Seibert at Antioch Community Church in Waco, Texas, to focus on just three core values – the 'core of the core', so to speak.

One day, while reading John 15, it occurred to me that Jesus passed on the values of the kingdom in the same shortened manner. Jesus emphasises three things:

- Abiding in Christ
- Loving each other
- Being witnesses to him

Obviously, there are many other values in the kngdom. But they all come back to these three: Love God; love each other; love those who don't know Jesus.

I teach, disciple, train, and witness around these truths. They can be expanded, of course, as there are many truths that make up the kingdom of God, but these three comprise the core of the kingdom.

Knowing and loving God. Loving and discipling other followers of Jesus. Reaching out to those who don't know Jesus. It makes it simple, but again, that doesn't mean it's easy. I have spent a lifetime learning what each of these truths mean and how they are to be worked out in my life and character. They are simple on the surface, but have great depth to explore and enjoy.

There is plenty of room for diversity in God's family. No doubt you have been led by God to other values and other ways of expressing your values: just find language that fits your church or movement.

My prayer is that you will experience the blessing of having a set of core values that resonate in your heart and unite your church and movement to move in power as you obey Jesus and live for his glory.

Appendix D

Recommended Books for Further Reading

Cole, Neil, *Organic Church*, Jossey-Bass (Wiley) 2005

Coleman, Robert, *The Master Plan of Evangelism*, Revell (Baker Book House) 1963, 1993

Garrison, David, *Church Planting Movements*, WIGTake Resources

Greig, Pete and Roberts, Dave, *Red Moon Rising*, Survivor Books (Kingsway) 2003

Hession, Roy, *The Calvary Road*, CLC 1950

Hirsch, Alan, *The Forgotten Ways*, Brazos (Baker Book House) 2006

Kreider, Larry, *The Cry for Spiritual Mothers and Fathers*, Dove Christian Fellowship International 2002

Kreider, Larry, and McClung, Floyd, *Starting a House Church*, Regal Books 2007

Kreider, Larry, et al, *The Biblical Role of Elders for Today's Church*, House to House Publications 2003

McClung, Floyd, *Basic Discipleship*, InterVarsity Press 1992

McClung, Floyd, *Living on the Devil's Doorstep*, YWAM (USA) and Paternoster Press (UK) 1988, 1999

McClung, Floyd, *The Father Heart of God*, Harvest House (USA) and Kingsway Publications (UK) 1985

Malphurs, Aubrey, *Values-Driven Leadership*, Baker Book House 1996

McClung, Floyd, *Finding Friendship with God*, YWAM 1993

Murray, Andrew, *Humility*, various publishers including CLC, Hendrickson, Whitaker House, Bethany House

Parrish, Ron, *From Duty to Delight*, Partnership Publications 2006

Piper, John, *Let the Nations Be Glad*, Baker Book House (USA) and Inter-Varsity Press (UK) 2003

Simson, Wolfgang, *Houses That Change the World*, Authentic Lifestyle 2001